The Almohad Movement in North Africa in the Twelfth and Thirteenth Centuries

The Almohad Movement in North Africa in the Twelfth and Thirteenth Centuries

ROGER LE TOURNEAU

PRINCETON UNIVERSITY PRESS
PRINCETON, NEW JERSEY
1969

L.C. Card No.: 68-27414

This book has been composed in Linotype Granjon

Printed in the United States of America
by Princeton University Press, Princeton, New Jersey

To the Memory of Georges Marçais

FOREWORD

In the fall of 1959 I gave three public lectures on the Almohad movement as part of the Class of 1932 Lectureship at Princeton University. Later, Professor T. Cuyler Young, Chairman of the Department of Oriental Languages at Princeton, asked me to prepare these lectures for publication. This allowed me to develop the subject further and to present it in a more scholarly way.

It is very gratifying to acknowledge here the kindness of Professor Young and the generosity of Princeton University. I want to add that Professor Bayly Winder, Mrs. Edward Sullivan, and Mrs. T. Cuyler Young were kind enough to revise my English text, and I am greatly indebted to them.

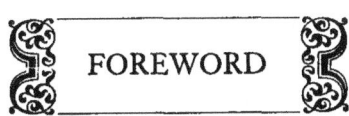

This book is a series of reflections on the Almohads, and is in no sense a history of the movement since such an enterprise has been undertaken many times, most recently by Señor Ambrosio Huici Miranda of Valencia in his two-volume, *Históría política del imperio almohade*, published in 1956-1959. My principal aim is to try to understand how the Almohads succeeded in uniting all of North Africa and Spain under their domination, and, in addition, why they failed to maintain this unity. Furthermore, the interest of such an inquiry is not a purely academic one since North African unity is a contemporary problem. I do not mean to say that what happened in the past will necessarily take place again along the same lines in the future and that North African unity can never be anything other than temporary and fragile; after all, the main factors and circumstances of the present period differ markedly from those of the Almohad period. I do think, however, that some essential factors are still in effect today that were operative in the twelfth century, and that consequently the eventual promoters of North African unity should meditate on the Almohad experience and avoid, if possible, some of the shortcomings of the Almohad rulers.

ROGER LE TOURNEAU

Princeton
Spring 1968

CONTENTS

Foreword vii

I. The Birth of a Movement 3

II. Building an Empire 48

III. Decay and Collapse 89

A Note on Sources and a List of Contemporary Accounts and Historical Studies 115

Index 123

The Almohad Movement in North Africa in the Twelfth and Thirteenth Centuries

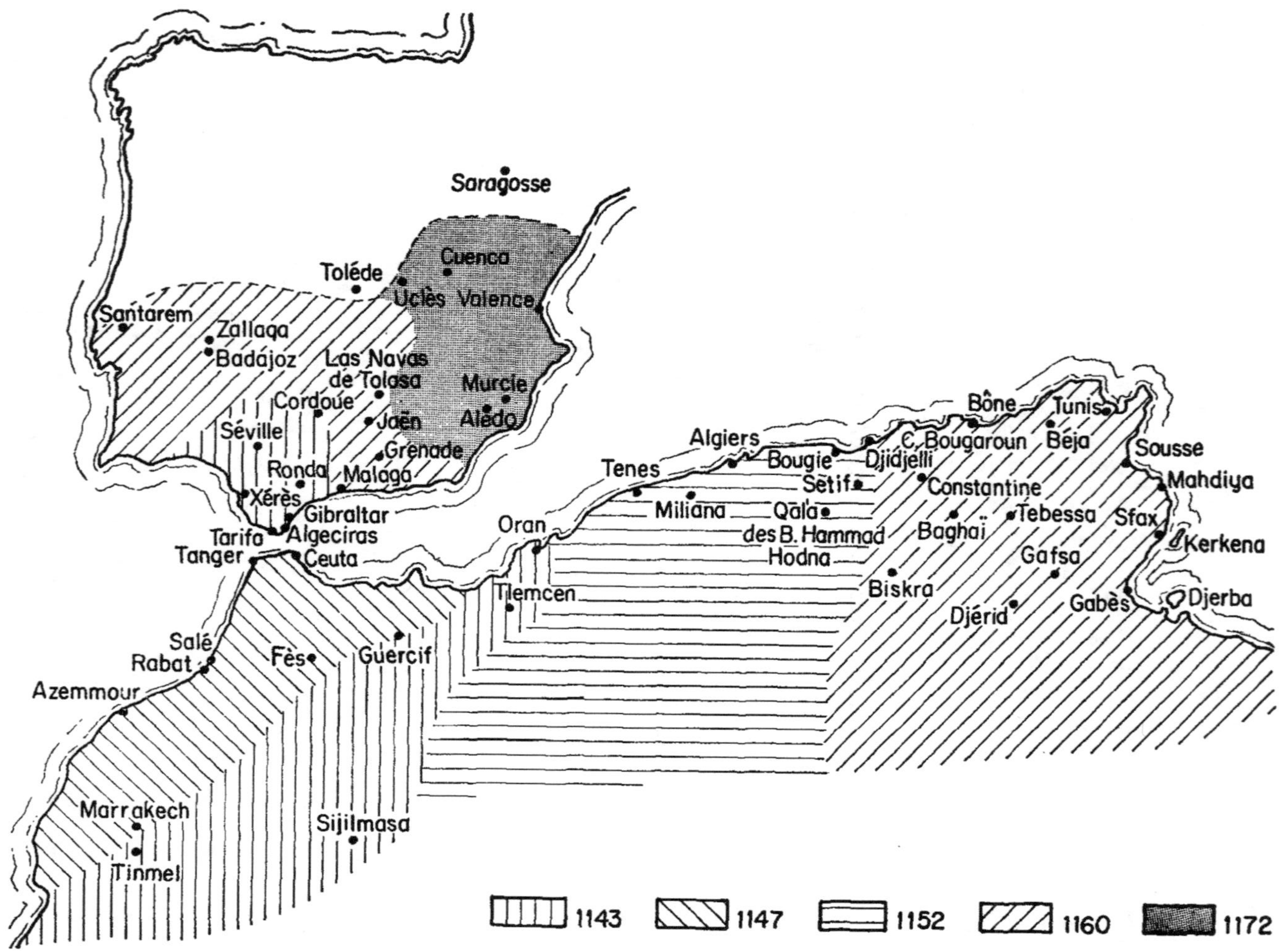

Saragosse
Cuenca
Tolède
Uclès
Valence
Santarem
Zallaqa
Badajoz
Las Navas
de Tolosa
Murcie
Cordoue
Aledo
Jaën
Séville
Grenade
Ronda
Malaga
Xérès
Gibraltar
Tarifa
Algeciras
Tanger
Ceuta
Oran
Tlemcen
Tenes
Miliana
Algiers
Bougie
Sétif
Qala
des B. Hammad
Hodna
Djidjelli
C. Bougaroun
Constantine
Bône
Baghaï
Tebessa
Biskra
Djérid
Tunis
Beja
Gafsa
Sousse
Mahdiya
Sfax
Kerkena
Gabès
Djerba
Salé
Rabat
Fès
Guercif
Azemmour
Marrakech
Sijilmasa
Tinmel
1143
1147
1152
1160
1172

CHAPTER ONE

THE BIRTH OF A MOVEMENT

PROBABLY during the year 1118—the chronology of these events is not very precise[1]—a Berber from southern Morocco, having left the Near East where he had spent years as a student in close contact with many distinguished scholars and philosophers, disembarked at Mahdiya in Ifrīqiya. Muhammad ibn 'Abd Allah Ibn Tūmart was returning to his fatherland full of new ideas and convinced that he had the mission of reforming Islam in the Maghrib. He was to initiate one of the most important ideological and political movements ever seen in that area, the movement of the unitarians, *al-muwaḥḥidūn.*

Ibn Tūmart was born in southern Morocco, probably on the northern slopes of the Anti-Atlas range, in a place called Igīllīz-n-Hargha, a village inhabited by some families of the Hargha tribe, itself a member of the wide Berber group of the Maṣmūḍa, commonly known now as Shleuh.[2] He was the son of a minor chieftain of the village, and genealogists later established that his family was related to that of the Prophet.[3] This may well be true since at the end of the eighth century several members of this noble family had come to the Maghrib in order to

[1] On the beginnings of Ibn Tūmart and a chronology, see Ambrosio Huici Miranda, *Historia política del imperio almohade* (Tetuán, 1956-59), I, pp. 23-38.

[2] *Ibid.*, p. 23.

[3] Evariste Lévi-Provençal, *Documents inédits d'histoire . . .* (Paris, 1928), text and translation; Miranda, *Historia política, op.cit.*, pp. 26-27.

escape the persecutions of the 'Abbāsids and, according to some chroniclers, some of them went as far as the Atlas Mountains. However, the Sherifian ancestry of Ibn Tūmart is not certain and may be unfounded. In any case, even if he had some drops of Sherifian blood in his veins, he was educated in a purely Berber environment and most of his ancestors were Maṣmūḍa.

The Maṣmūḍa Berbers have been carefully studied[4] because they form an original and homogeneous community. As they do today, they occupied, toward the end of the eleventh century, the western half of the High Atlas range, from the Atlantic Ocean to the Tadla regions, and the whole Anti-Atlas range. They were divided into a number of political units of unequal importance: confederations, tribes, or fractions.

The Maṣmūḍa have continued to the present day to keep pure their Berber language, their political organizations, and probably their judicial customs and their family patterns. They had, moreover, adhered to Islam for some time, perhaps since 'Uqba ibn Nafi' had traversed those regions at the end of the seventh century,[5] or from the time several descendants of the Prophet in order to escape the menace of the Oriental 'Abbāsids came to the mountain ranges of southern Morocco in search of a refuge,[6] or pos-

[4] Robert Montagne, *Les Berbères et le Makhzen dans le Sud du Maroc* (Paris, 1930); Jacques Berque, *Structures sociales du Haut Atlas* (Paris, 1955).

[5] Evariste Lévi-Provençal, "Un nouveau récit de la conquête de l'Afrique du Nord par les Arabes," *Arabica*, 1 (1954), 38-39.

[6] Rawḍ al-Qirṭās, *Annales regum Mauritaniae* . . . , C. J. Tornberg, ed. (Upsala, 1843-46), pp. 4/5 (the first page number is that of the Arabic text and the second that of Tornberg's Latin translation).

sibly dating from the year 197/813 when Idrīs ibn Idrīs established his power over them.[7] Their Islamism was deeply rooted in their souls, but lacked doctrine and laws —an Islam that had appealed more to the hearts than it had modified the mores.

At the time Ibn Tūmart was born, the Maṣmūḍa lived under the theoretical rule of the Almoravids, but seem to have enjoyed what would be called today a status of internal autonomy, with one exception—the Almoravid ruler would from time to time send a military expedition to the Maghrib to collect taxes, and the Almoravid soldiers would behave as if they had entered a conquered country.[8] There is no indication, however, that a feeling of rebellion against the current power had arisen in the minds of the Maṣmūḍa before Ibn Tūmart returned to them after his stay in the Orient, nor had they felt any restlessness about their way of practicing their Islamic faith.

The date of Ibn Tūmart's birth is not clear—dates as far apart as 1077 and 1097 have been given by various chroniclers—but summarizing all the information available, as did Señor Huici Miranda, we may assume the date of his birth to be near 1080.

We do not know anything precise about his childhood, except that Ibn Tūmart was a very pious and studious boy. In 1106 or later he started "seeking knowledge," as the Arabic phrase expresses it, and he probably spent some time in Cordova. He then set out by sea to the

[7] *Ibid.*, pp. 27/39, where the Maṣmūḍa are nominally designated.

[8] Ibn al-Aṯīr, *Kāmil fi 'ta'rīkh*, C. J. Tornberg, ed. (Leiden, 1867-84), x, pp. 403-04; de Slane, trans., pp. 573-74.

Muslim East, where it is certain that he spent as much as ten years. This kind of behavior was not common among the Berbers of the Extreme West, as Morocco was called at that time; however, some years later, another young Berber, ʿAbd al-Mūʾmin was on the point of doing the same thing, if we can trust the chroniclers, when he met Ibn Tūmart, as we shall see later. One may conjecture that Ibn Tūmart, when he started on his way to the Orient, wanted only to become a learned man. It is certain, however, that when he came back to the Maghrib he considered himself to have been given a mission —religious reform. Al-Marrākushī, one of the chroniclers of the Almohad period, and some others, show him acting as a reformer of morals in Alexandria and even on the boat, returning to the Maghrib.[9] We would like to know in detail the evolution of Ibn Tūmart's thought during his sojourn in Egypt and Syria, but we have only limited and sometimes contradictory information. For instance, some chroniclers say, on the authority of eye-witnesses, that he met al-Ghazzālī in Baghdad and received from him the mission of overthrowing the Almoravids, then masters of Morocco; others, like Ibn al-Aṯīr, a very well-informed historian of the thirteenth century, affirm categorically that there never was such a meeting. The following passage is a translation of the anonymous chronicle, *Al-ḥulal al-mawshiyya*, where the point is treated:

> This has been reported by Ibn Ṣāḥib al-Salāt from ʿAbd Allah ibn ʿAbd al-Rāḥman al-ʿIraqi, a very old

[9] Al-Marrākushī, *The History of the Almohades*, Dozy, ed. (Leiden, 1881), p. 129; trans., p. 156.

man of Fez, "I was in Baghdad," said he, "in the school of the shaykh, the imām Abū Ḥāmid al-Ghazzālī, when an old man, thick-bearded and wearing a wool turban came in; he entered the school, went to the shaykh Abū Ḥāmid and saluted him: 'Whence is this man?' said the shaykh. He answered: 'From the Extreme West.'

'Did you go to Cordova?'

'Yes.'

'How are the theologians there?'

'Well.'

'Did they receive the Book of the Revival [*Kitāb Iḥyā' 'Ulūm al-Dīn*, the main work of al-Ghazzālī]?'

'Yes.'

'And what did they say about it?'

Then the old man, ill at ease, kept silent; the imām besought him to answer. The other shook his head and told how the book had been burned and what had happened. 'Then,' says the witness, 'the imām changed countenance, stretched his arms in a gesture of invocation and, while the students said amen, said these words: "May their empire fly into pieces, as they destroyed this book, and may their dynasty disappear as they burnt it."'

Abū 'Abd Allāh Ibn Tūmart al-Sūsī, later called the Mahdī, began to speak so: 'O imām, ask God that He commit this task to my hands.' But al-Ghazzālī did not pay attention to him. Some days later, another old man, exactly like the former, went to the assembly. The shaykh Abū Ḥāmid questioned him and he confirmed the exactitude of the former report; the shaykh invoked

God as he had done previously. Then the Mahdī told him: 'Their fate will be in my hands if God wills.'

'O God,' said al-Ghazzālī, 'commit their fate to his hands.'

God listened to this prayer. Abū 'Abd Allāh Ibn Tūmart left Baghdad and set out to the Maghrib, knowing that the shaykh's prayer would not be in vain."[10]

I at first had the impression that this testimony was authentic and that Ibn Tūmart in fact had, through the influence of al-Ghazzālī, a sudden revelation of a political mission in the Maghrib and had returned to his native land with the intention of overthrowing the Almoravid dynasty.[11] After reflection, however, I have come to the conclusion that I was mistaken. I had not paid enough attention to the literary character of the chronicler's description of the episode, to the extraordinary and too perfect coincidence of two old men coming from Spain just a few days apart, and to the theatrical apostrophe of al-Ghazzālī against the Almoravids. All that is much too well arranged to be true. Moreover, when Ibn Tūmart first returned to the Maghrib, he did not immediately behave as an enemy of the Almoravids, but acted purely and simply as a reformer of morals and as a theologian.

[10] *Al-Ḥulal al-mawshiyya,* I. S. Allouche, ed. (Rabat, 1936), pp. 85-86. Translation is mine; compare with Huici Miranda's *Colección de crónicas árabes de la reconquista,* I (Tetuán, 1952), pp. 125-26.

[11] Roger Le Tourneau, "Al-Ghazali et Ibn Toumert se sont-ils recontrés?," *Bulletin des Etudes Arabes.* On the subject, see the objections of Huici Miranda, *La leyenda y al historia en los origenes del imperio almohade, Al-Andalus,* XIV (1949), 342-45.

Far from dashing to the Almoravid territory, he spent some months, perhaps years, in the eastern part of North Africa which was not under the authority of the Almoravids. If he had been convinced that he had been invested with a sort of divine mission to drive them away, he would have followed a different course. It seems, therefore, that the above testimony must be rejected, as well as the idea that al-Ghazzālī is responsible for the political vocation of Ibn Tūmart.

In any case, his long stay in Egypt and Syria certainly served as the basis for his future behavior. There he found himself in a stimulating intellectual atmosphere. The great theological disputes of the previous centuries had left traces; the Ash'arite school of theology which had finally prevailed was still in full vigor. If Ibn Tūmart was neither a student of al-Ghazzālī nor a follower of his doctrine, he obviously had heard of it. One may easily imagine the great activity of Ibn Tūmart's mind. He would unceasingly compare what he saw and heard in the Orient with the poverty and rusticity of Islam in the West, particularly in his native Morocco, concluding that the situation there must be completely modified and that he would be the instrument of that modification. I am convinced, however, that he came to this idea little by little and that he thought about it in terms of morals and perhaps of theology, but not yet in terms of politics. I am not able to discover that he showed a political attitude before his arrival in Marrakesh.

Therefore, the picture presented by the chroniclers of Ibn Tūmart being seized by a sudden revelation (like Saint Paul on his way to Damascus) and feeling himself invested with a political and religious mission, such as it is depicted by many chroniclers favorable or not to the Mahdī, seems very far from reality.

Nevertheless what remains true is that Ibn Tūmart was profoundly influenced by his journey in the Orient and came back with the conviction that Islam in the Maghrib, and particularly in Morocco, was not what it ought to be. If he did not come back from the Orient as a political revolutionist, he came back as a reformer of mores and doctrine, and was probably convinced that it was his duty to bring such a reform to a successful conclusion and he was the only man able to do so.

Such was, it seems to me, the state of mind of the future Mahdī when he embarked on the return voyage to his native country. It is unlikely that he at that time had worked out a precise plan of action since he had been away for a long time and hardly knew what was happening in his native land. But it seems clear that he considered himself as called by God to turn his Berber brethren to the "right path," as is said in the Koran. This conviction does not seem to be the result of any particular external influence, that of al-Ghazzālī for instance, but of a long internal evolution, the result of all he had seen and heard during his years in the Orient. It is regrettable that some clarifying information on this period in Ibn Tūmart's life is not available, but the first section of al-Baiḏaq's book, which might have been helpful, was either lost or, more likely, the author, being a simple man, was unable to trace adequately the development of the thought of such a man as the Mahdī.

Furthermore it does not seem that Ibn Tūmart's movement was the answer to a deep call from the Berber population. Nothing, as I have already emphasized, allows one to think that the Berbers under Almoravid rule suffered from a spiritual uneasiness. At most they found that the dominant Almoravids sometimes made attacks upon their freedom, but in a no more aggressive manner than did the various reigns which succeeded each other in Morocco.

Ibn Tūmart, of course, did find some favorable conditions which he knew how to exploit, but one may safely say that they were not a decisive factor. They played their role only as a result of Ibn Tūmart's initiative.

One may therefore conclude that at the beginning the Almohad movement received its impetus from the spiritual evolution of a single man and his unswerving will to accomplish the mission that he had undertaken.

Ibn Tūmart probably landed at Mahdīya in a Maghrib which had never known political unity, except for some thirty years at the beginning of the Arab conquest. After the arrival of the Arab Bedouins in 1051, the eastern part of the Maghrib, Ifrīqiya, was divided into several small principalities, some of which were ruled by Arab and some by Berber families. The kingdom of the Ḥammādids, a Berber dynasty established in the central Maghrib at the beginning of the eleventh century, was in its turn threatened by the Bedouins, and the rulers decided to transfer their capital from al-Qal'a of the Banī Ḥammād to Bougie (Bijaya) in 1091, practically abandoning the southern part of their territory to the Bedouins.

The Almoravid empire, created some fifty years before by a group of Berber tribes of the western Sahara, was a stable and brilliant civilization flourishing to the west of the Ḥammādid kingdom.[12] Under the command of a highly able man, Yūsuf ibn Tāshfīn, they had conquered the western half of the Maghrib and the whole of Moslem Spain. Shortly thereafter, these rude Berber camel-breeders were transformed under Spanish influence, at least with regard to their elite, into a highly educated people, fond of Spanish poetry, of Spanish architecture, and of Spanish luxury, in a word, of Spanish civilization, and they did not spare any effort to bring it to the Maghrib where it had made a timid appearance at the end of the tenth century.

The Almoravid empire was not the largest Muslim state set up in North Africa: under the Umaiyad caliphate, the whole of North Africa and nearly the entire Spanish peninsula had been unified under single rule; later on, in the tenth century, the Fatimids had reigned over the greater part of the Maghrib, but until the end of the eleventh century, the Berbers had never succeeded in creating so large a political community under the sign of Islam. The former empires had been set up by conquerors from abroad who had imposed their rule. It is evident that the Kutāma had helped the Fatimids in establishing and in maintaining their authority, but they had been mere tools in the hands of masters from the Orient who had conceded to their Berber auxiliaries some of the benefits of power and certain honors, although they had not let them participate in the use of authority.

As for the Almoravids, they were genuine Berbers who without help had built up their empire with their own hands. ‘Abd Allah ibn Yāsīn, the religious founder of the

[12] On the Amoravids, see Henri Terrasse, *Histoire du Maroc*, (Casablanca, 1949), 1, pp. 211-60.

Almoravid movement, Abū Bakr ibn 'Umar, the first Almoravid chief who had conquered the southern part of Morocco, and Yūsuf ibn Tāshfīn, who had extended Almoravid power to Algiers in one direction and Saragoza in the other, were Ṣanhāja Berbers, born and educated in a Berber environment.

However, the Almoravid power contained in itself a germ of weakness. When the tribes coming from the Sahara settled in the Maghrib and Spain, they did not allow the Berber tribes which they had subdued by sheer force to join in their victory. The Zanāta, who had established their authority over a great part of the country, were considered by the Ṣanhāja as rivals, perhaps hereditary rivals if one admits that a racial antagonism had set these two groups in opposition, and they were dealt with as rivals. The Barghawāṭa,[13] treated as heretics, were exterminated as such. It should be noted that the Zanāta and the Barghawāṭa formed two important Berber groups in Morocco and western Algeria. As for other Berbers (the Maṣmūḍa for instance) who were not subjugated, they were nonetheless reduced to the rank of subjects, according to tradition. In any case the Spanish Muslims, although they enjoyed a brilliant and refined civilization and many of them participated as technicians in building up the Almoravid empire, were treated in their own country as a conquered people and exposed to the mercy of Almoravid soldiers and to vexatious measures.[14]

No evidence shows that the Berbers, dominated by Almoravid rule, fostered rebellious ideas, but one may

[13] *Encyclopedia of Islam*, 2nd edn., I, p. 1075.

[14] Evariste Lévi-Provençal, *Séville musulmane au XIIe siècle* (Paris, 1947), pp. 61-62.

imagine they felt some dissatisfaction when they saw the Ṣanhāja of the desert governing alone and behaving in a patronizing way to anyone who was not a member of their victorious group. We may then safely assume that they were ready to follow anyone who would oppose the Almoravid masters.

At that time, however brilliant the Almoravid civilization was, it was in some ways unstable, for this beautiful flower had grown too fast and was fragile. Aside from the sophisticated rulers, most of the Almoravids and the rest of the Moroccan population were still primitive, and the split grew wider between the elite and the bulk of the population. On the other hand, even the Almoravid rulers were prisoners of their religious origins. They had conquered Morocco in the name of the faith, convinced that they had the mission of reforming Islam in that country, and consequently they had granted considerable authority to the doctors of the law, the *fuqahā'*. The *fuqahā'* were imbued with the narrow principles of the Maliki school of law and thus were guided by the letter and not by the spirit of the Koran, showing themselves to be extremely formalist. They had been led at the beginning of the twelfth century to burn in public the book of al-Ghazzālī on the *Revival of Religious Sciences*, considering it a pack of heresies.[15] Finally, after 1106, the Almoravid kingdom was ruled by a son of Yūsuf ibn Tāshfīn, 'Ali ibn Yūsuf, a very pious man, well-educated and fond of Spanish civilization, but devoid of will and completely under the influence of the narrow-minded *fuqahā'*.[16] In brief, behind the beautiful façade of the Almoravid empire lay

[15] On that point, see, among others, al-Marrākushī, *op.cit.*, p. 123.
[16] *Ibid.*

a society in transition, and the different parts, assembled by the decree of Yūsuf ibn Tāshfīn, did not fit together very well.

After his disembarkation, Ibn Tūmart started without haste on his way to the West with three companions, Berbers like himself, among whom was al-Baiḏaq, the author of our main source on Ibn Tūmart's beginnings. Before arriving in Bougie, Ibn Tūmart apparently stopped in many places and openly taught and tried to reform the mores. In Bougie, scandalized by the luxury and the laxity of the morals there, he did his utmost to correct what he considered sinful abuses, even using violence at times.

What he considered reprehensible was public behavior that he could readily observe and penalize: in Bougie the chroniclers point out[17] the clothes of the women were gaudy and luxurious, some of the men wore feminine clothes, the sexes mingled in the streets on the occasion of religious festivals, and wine was sold publicly. Later on, in Fez, he turned his attention to musical instruments and commanded his disciples to destroy them in quantity.[18] He tried at first to demonstrate to the people that they were guilty of wrongdoing and he worked very hard to bring them willingly back to the right path. If they did not pay attention to his objurgations, he did not hesitate to chastise them with a stick when he judged their behavior contrary to the proper functioning of Muslim so-

[17] Evariste Lévi-Provençal, "Six fragments d'une chronique anonyme du début des Almohades," in *Mélanges René Basset*, II (Paris, 1925), pp. 347-48 (text), 374-75 (trans.); *Documents inédits*, pp. 52/78-80.

[18] *Documents inédits*, pp. 64-65/101.

ciety. His attitude and actions in Bougie caused some reactions and the authorities requested him to leave the city. Perhaps even he understood that the unwholesome atmosphere at Bougie was too pervading for him to accomplish anything by singlehandedly putting people to shame and using violence against the unrepentant among them. Only long and exacting work could possibly bring about the desired result and he therefore willingly left Bougie. He chose next to teach in the small village of Mellāla, a few miles away from Bougie on the left bank of the Summān River, and there he built an oratory, welcomed some disciples, and in general behaved as if he planned to remain a long time. It seems clear from this that he did not at this time intend to start political action against the Almoravids since he buried himself in such a remote place and would be unable to make any purposeful moves from Mellāla. It appears that reformation of the mores at Bougie was his primary concern and his full goal at this time.

It was at Mellāla that he met the man who was to be his successor and the true founder of the Almohad empire, 'Abd al-Mū'min ibn 'Alī, a native of the coastal range of Trāra, west of Oran. This meeting between the two leaders is treated as providential by nearly all chroniclers. Al-Baiḏaq who claimed to have been an eye-witness of the meeting reported on the episode and his account seems to be the most authentic. Al-Baiḏaq relates that 'Abd al-Mū'min was traveling to the Orient with one of his uncles and, having come to Bougie, heard of Ibn Tūmart and wished to see him; his uncle allowed him to go to Mellāla for this purpose.

'Abd al-Mū'min hastened to the Imām. On his way, he joined students, walked with them and at last arrived at the mosque's gate. The Infallible [Ibn Tūmart] raised his head, while 'Abd al-Mū'min was standing before him, and told him: "Come in, young man." He came in and was to sit down among the people, but the Infallible Imām repeatedly invited him to come close to him, so that at last he was near him. The Imām asked him: "What is your name, young man? 'Abd al-Mū'min. Your father is 'Alī? Yes." People who were there were astonished. He went on: "Where have you come from? From the province of Tlemcen, from the coastal region of Kūmiya. Is it not from Tājra?" said the Imām.

"Yes."

The astonishment of the company was increasing. Then he went on: "Where are you going to, young man?"

"To the Orient, master, to seek knowledge."

"This knowledge which you wish to acquire in the Orient, you have just found it in the Occident."

After the meeting, people went away; the future caliph ('Abd al-Mū'min) also made ready to depart but the Imām told him: "You will spend the night with us, young man." He accepted the *faqīh*'s invitation. Thus he spent the night in our home. When darkness fell, the Imām took 'Abd al-Mū'min's hand and they went. In the middle of the night, the Infallible called me: "Abū Bakr, give me the book which is in the red case." I gave it and he added: "Light the lamp." Thus he began to read the book to this man who was to be caliph after him; while I stood holding the lamp, I heard him say: "The mission on which depends the life of the religion will succeed only by 'Abd al-Mū'min, the torch of the Almohades."

The future caliph, when he heard those words, began to shed tears and said: "O *faqīh*, I am not at all qualified for such a role; I am only a man who seeks that which will purify him from his sins."

"The thing that will purify you from your sins," answered the Infallible, "will be the part you will play in the reformation of this world." And he gave him the book, saying: "Happy are those of whom you will be the chief and woe to those who will oppose you from the first to the last. Repeat frequently Allah's name; may He bless you all your life, may He guide you in the right way, may He shelter you against whatever might bring you fear and apprehension."

Then the Infallible told me: "Abū Bakr, call the disciples for the *wird* [spiritual exercise]. Let them get up and recite their part of the Koran." When they were present, he addressed them as follows: "Certainly Allah only is one God. The Prophet is truth, the Mahdī is truth and the caliph is truth. Read Abū Dawud's *hadith* [tradition]. You will know what he says about that. Your Lord deserves your obedience and submissiveness. Salute." They made their spiritual prayer and recited the Koran.

In the morning, Ya'lū, the future caliph's uncle, came in and told his nephew: " 'Abd al-Mū'min, do you intend to delay us any more and let the boats sail without us?"

"The knowledge he wished to acquire in the Orient,"

answered the master, "it came to him here in the Maghrib. Yield to Allah's and the Imām's will."

Abd al-Mū'min studied under him; he was the most intelligent of his disciples. When he desired to sleep, the Infallible asked him: "How can he whom the world is waiting for, sleep?" Some months went on like that.[19]

Ibn Khaldūn, however, says that 'Abd al-Mū'min, who was at that moment a student in Tlemcen, was sent to Ibn Tūmart by his fellow students to ask him to replace one of their teachers who had just died. This constitutes proof of at least two things: first, that Ibn Tūmart's fame was spreading far and wide, and, second that he was in Mellāla for rather a long time since the means of communication was extremely slow at that time and a long interval was needed for fame to spread in such a manner.

It is very difficult to know which account to accept—al-Baiḏaq's with its providential feature or Ibn Khaldūn's more rational explanation. A modern historian feels tempted to fall in with Ibn Khaldūn's interpretation because it appears more credible, and Ibn Khaldūn rightly enjoys a great prestige among Westerners. But we must not forget that he wrote two centuries and a half after the events and his documentation on the Almohad period was full of serious gaps.

Al-Baiḏaq certainly did not have the same intellectual capacity as Ibn Khaldūn; in many cases he appears credulous and single-minded. Moreover, it is certain that he wrote his testimony very late, under the reign of 'Abd al-Mū'min, when time could have blurred or even distorted his memories. But the event was so important and striking

[19] *Ibid.*, pp. 55-57/85-88.

that it inevitably left a strong impression on his simple mind; he gives many precise details and asserts that he was an eye-witness of the facts he describes so that we are inclined to be prudent. In short I think it would be unwise to ignore al-Baiḏaq's account and to trust Ibn Khaldūn's. One may question some details, but the general outline of al-Baiḏaq's testimony should be given serious consideration.

Up to this time Ibn Tūmart does not seem to have had any political preoccupations: he teaches, he tries to induce or oblige people to behave according to the Law, or rather to a strict interpretation of the Law. In short, Ibn Tūmart conducts himself as a champion of the Law, valid in any place and at any time, against the local custom. Centuries later, 'Allāl al-Fāsī will assume the same attitude in twentieth century Morocco; but his position is less surprising than Ibn Tūmart's, since he was not educated, as Ibn Tūmart was, in a Berber environment under the influence of local custom. It is probable that originally there may have been a conflict in the mind of Ibn Tūmart, but, recognizing that the Law must logically supplant custom, he silenced his own doubts, controlled his ancestral habits, and thereby made himself a champion of the Law.

If he leaves Mellāla, is it only to answer the call of the students of Tlemcen? Strict account must be taken on this point of al-Baiḏaq's report which is unfortunately his alone and which remains full of mystery. "One day," he writes immediately after the previous testimony,[20] "came two men on their way to the Orient; one's name was 'Abd Allah ibn 'Abd al-'Azīz, and the other's 'Abd-al-Ṣamad

[20] *Ibid.*, pp. 57/88.

ibn 'Abd al-Ḥalīm. Interrogated by the Imām, they answered that they had come from the Maghrib, and they were disconcerted by their experiences. Then al-Baiḏaq said to the two travelers: 'Why do you not speak?' They replied in their language, 'We do not understand Arabic.' And they added: 'O *faqīh*, we come from the Atlas province, from Tīnmallāl.' He questioned them in their language, invoked God in their favor and they departed. When the night came, the master told us: 'Make ready to depart for the Maghrib, if God wills. There is neither strength nor power if not in God.' "

It is not certain that this meeting was decisive, although nothing else explains the sudden departure of Ibn Tūmart who was comfortably settled in Mellāla at that time. One is led, however, to state the issue and to build up an assumption on the description of the visit of those two Berbers—an event which left such a precise memory in the mind of al-Baiḏaq. Would they not have, by their own account, suddenly caused ideas to develop in Ibn Tūmart's mind which up to that time were only beginning to take shape? Did not Ibn Tūmart at that time begin to think that political action against the Almoravids was possible in Morocco and that, in any case, he must go and learn on the spot what the situation was?

What is certain and follows the same line as the above-mentioned assumption is that after having left Mellāla, Ibn Tūmart seemed anxious to reach his native country quickly while previously he had not hesitated to stop on his way for long periods. Nevertheless, when he is in the territory ruled by the Almoravids he does not restrain himself from remonstrating with officials and attempting to induce them to reverse decisions that he considers unlawful: at Garsīf he obliges a vizier to make restitution of a collective fine which he had imposed on the population because one of his ostriches had been killed; for that purpose he goes directly to the Almoravid in command of the place and succeeds in being heard. In Fez, according to one chronicler,[21] he was expelled by the governor on the instigation of several doctors of the law whom he had prevailed over in a dogmatic controversy. Later on he did not hesitate to face the Almoravid sovereign himself. In short, he acquires greater and greater confidence in himself and begins to consider his spiritual ministry equal at least to the vizier's and governor's temporal power. Is that so very different from being persuaded that this temporal power must be subject to the spiritual ministry and should gradually be replaced by it?

We are inclined to believe that Ibn Tūmart's inward conviction asserted itself as he meditated, but also that the reception given him by the young and by many pious people (if al-Baiḏaq's account is to be trusted),[22] added to his resolution. He probably became persuaded that many people were waiting for his message and would follow him wherever he would lead them.

At last he arrived in Marrakesh and there he deliberately clashed with the Almoravid officials and indeed with the sovereign himself whom he admonished publicly.

[21] Al-Marrākushī, *History, op.cit.*, pp. 132/160.

[22] This welcome is attested in Mellāla where the future Mahdī has around him a circle of disciples, in Tlemcen, in Oujda, on the way between Taza and Fez, in Fez itself where al Baiḏaq gives the names of fourteen assiduous disciples, in Meknès, where he cites eleven disciples, in Salé where a *cadi* was among his audience.

"When he arrived in Marrakesh," reports al-Baiḏaq,[23] "he settled there in the mosque of *Ṣawma'at al-tūb* [the earthen minaret] and he remained there until the following Friday. Then he went to the mosque of 'Alī ibn Yūsuf and found 'Alī ibn Yūsuf [the Almoravid sovereign] sitting on Ibn Taizamt's[24] mat, with his viziers standing next to him. They told Ibn Tūmart: 'Salute the ameer by his title of caliph,' 'Where is the ameer,' he answered. 'I only see slave-girls with veils.' When he heard that, 'Alī ibn Yūsuf put off the veil from his face, telling them, 'He is right.' When he saw him [unveiled], the Infallible said, 'The caliphate is Allah's and not yours, 'Alī ibn Yūsuf.' Then he added, 'Rise up from this dyed thing and you will be an imām of justice and do not sit on this dyed mat.' 'Alī put aside the mat, gave it to its owner and said, 'What about the dyeing?' Ibn Tūmart replied, 'Because when it was used, it was mixed with droppings.' "

Struck by this extraordinary man, 'Alī ibn Yūsuf wanted to get more information about him and arranged a meeting between him and some Almoravid theologians, among whom was Ibn Wuhaib, a scholar born in Sevilla. During the debate, Ibn Tūmart showed himself superior to his opponents. As a result, Ibn Wuhaib became greatly irritated and requested the sovereign to have Ibn Tūmart arrested. 'Alī was on the point of ordering it when two Almoravid dignitaries intervened—why, none of the chroniclers explain—and managed to change the punishment to banishment from the city. He then settled in a ceme-

[23] *Documents inédits*, pp. 67-68/108-09.

[24] This man was probably one of the close collaborators of the sovereign, but we do not know anything more about him.

tery, claiming that there he was no longer on the sovereign's territory but on that of the dead. However, even those who had intervened in his favor requested him to scoff no longer at the prince's authority; he then started to go toward the Atlas range.[25]

At about this time Ibn Tūmart's thoughts became clear; he wanted the Almoravids to live according to his conception of Moslem law. If they did not agree to follow his advice, he would oppose them, but how? He probably had no definite idea on this point, but from the information he had gathered on his journey, he probably had the impression that he might rely on the Maṣmūḍa tribes of the High Atlas. Before drawing up a plan, however, he had to sound out the feelings of these tribal groups. Therefore, as soon as he felt that he was no longer safe at Marrakesh, he went to the Atlas Mountains and traveled through them for months, attracting various followers, including Abū Ḥafṣ 'Umar Intī, who would play such an important role in building up the Almohad empire.[26] It appears, however, that only a few individuals had now joined forces with him but no tribes followed his teaching and he therefore understood that the time had not yet come to launch an open rebellion against the Almoravids. Consequently, he settled down in his birthplace of Igīllīz and proceeded to send emissaries to the Maṣmūḍa tribes to prepare for what he surely now had in mind—the overthrow of the Almoravid empire. Nevertheless, the Almoravids were unable to accept his teach-

[25] *Documents inédits*, pp. 68-69/109-11.

[26] On this journey through the Atlas range, from the vicinity of Marrakesh to the ocean, see *Documents inédits*, pp. 70-72/112-16.

ings and reform their own beliefs and mores to conform with Ibn Tūmart's doctrine.

In his proselytizing, he strongly emphasized the Islamic theory of the Mahdī, that is, the doctrine that a man would be sent to earth by God just before the end of time in order to unite humanity under the law of Islam and prepare for its final destiny. As a result of his preaching he was proclaimed Mahdī by his early companions near the end of the year 1121, and later he was accepted by some Berber tribes of South Morocco. The fact is reported as follows by a chronicler of the fourteenth century who used earlier sources:

> One day he stood up to preach and said, "Praise to God Who does according to His will and accomplishes what He pleases. Nobody opposes His orders nor modifies His commands. May God bless our lord Muḥammad, God's messenger, who announced the coming of the imām, the Mahdī who will fill the earth with justice and equity as it has been filled with tyranny and oppression. God will send him to obliterate lies by truth and to replace tyranny with justice. The Extreme West is his place, and his time will be the last of times. . . ."
>
> "When the imām ended his speech," said the caliph 'Abd al-Mū'min, "ten of his followers rushed to him. I was one of them. We told him: 'O lord, these qualities may be found only in you: you are the Mahdī.' And we recognized him as such immediately afterwards even as the Prophet had been recognized by his companions. We swore to be a single corps for attack and defense." His ten companions recognized him as the

> Mahdī under a carob tree, and were followed by the Berbers who recognized him in their turn and swore that they would fight for him and dedicate their lives to his service. Although he let them know that this would involve risks, tests, struggles, and revolts, they worked hard at it. After that, his companions gave him the name of Mahdī.[27]

At the same time that he won veneration from the Berbers, by way of Mahdism, of some elementary doctrinal statements, and of objurgations of a moral character—he influenced them from within. Having come back to his native country, he well knew its weaknesses, which he tried to remedy, but he also knew its intricacies, its subtleties, and its secret motives. According to nearly all the chroniclers, he had not forgotten his mother tongue and used it to perfection. His tribe of the Hargha held no secrets for him, nor did the neighboring tribes; moreover, his later actions show that he had no difficulty in knowing and understanding the situation among the tribes of the High Atlas. He had never lived there before and this proves the fundamental unity of the Maṣmūḍa tribes.

I do not wish to minimize the ability of Ibn Tūmart's doctrine to influence the thinking of large numbers of people; it was great and certainly played an important role in the growing success of the man. But the apostle was nonetheless a native of the country who by his intimate knowledge of the situation and the people, by his skillfulness, and, let us be frank, his scheming mind, knew how to take advantage of any situation, especially

[27] *Al-Ḥulal al-mawshiyya, op.cit.*, pp. 87-88; my translation.

a local one, with a view to insinuating himself into his countrymen's good graces. One of Ibn Tūmart's most remarkable qualities was his capacity for combining into a compelling whole the doctrinal knowledge he had acquired in the Orient, the ideal of religious reform which he promoted and to which he was sincerely devoted, and his deep understanding of the country in which he was born.

The Almoravids heard of his preaching and of its success among the Berbers; as a consequence they tried to eradicate this new religious and political movement and sent troops to Igīllīz. In every case, Ibn Tūmart escaped the Almoravid army, sometimes at the last moment, with the help of a growing number of Berber chieftains, among whom was Abū Ḥafṣ 'Umar Intī. But he soon decided that he was not safe in Igīllīz and went, probably in 1124, to a place called Tinmel or Tīnmallāl, in the heart of the High Atlas, in the upper reaches of the Nfīs Valley.

There the Almohad movement was really fully developed by Ibn Tūmart and his disciples, though the latter were mere instruments in the hands of the master, who was the animating spirit of the new group. Tinmel, a small village in a narrow valley toward which other small valleys converged, was inhabited by Maṣmūḍa tribes, and the new religious community was perfectly safe there. The Almoravids had never truly ruled over that region because their soldiers, mostly horsemen, felt uncomfortable in such mountainous country, and in addition it was extremely easy for the Berbers to close the narrow, high, and difficult mountain passes leading to Tinmel. Ibn

Tūmart was now established in a natural and impregnable fortress,[28] and was in a position to propagate his doctrine among the Berber tribes around him. For that purpose, he seems to have organized a group of missionaries who went to the remotest tribes of the mountains[29] and preached to the people in the Berber language.

But what can we really say about Ibn Tūmart's doctrine?[30] His religious ideas are known to us through writings presented as his and gathered in a late twelfth century manuscript which was published in 1903 by a French scholar of Algiers, Jean-Dominique Luciani, under the title, *Le Livre d'Ibn Tūmart.* The main features of that doctrine, if I may say so, have no originality whatsoever—the author unceasingly proclaims God's unity and immateriality, together with the absolute necessity of complying with His commands. What is original in this are not the ideas themselves, but the desire to purify the Islamic doctrine corrupted by the times and to bring this about through the only true sources of Islamic faith—the Koran and the Prophet's tradition. At the same time at least some elements of theology were brought to the Muslims. If he had not tried to initiate the Moroccan masses to Islamic theology, which is an Ash'arite conception, and if the idea of the Mahdī had not appeared, one would have difficulty understanding why Ibn Tūmart was considered

[28] For a description of Tinmel, see Henri Basset and Henri Terrasse, *Sanctuaires et forteresses almohades* (Paris, 1932), pp. 1-8.

[29] Al-Marrākushī, *History, op.cit.*, pp. 134/162.

[30] On Ibn Tūmart's doctrine, see I. Goldziher's *Le Livre de Mohammed ibn Toumert . . .* ; "Materialien zur Kenntniss der Almohaden Bewegung," Z D M G, XLI (1887); Introduction to *Le Livre d'ibn Toumert, op.cit.*, pp. 1-102.

a *khārijī*, or heretic, by many of his contemporaries.[31] The concept of a Mahdī is orthodox in itself, but what is unorthodox—a Shī'ī idea—is that the Mahdī is infallible, and this is one of the basic principles of Ibn Tūmart's teachings.

When we read the *Livre d'Ibn Tūmart*, in which ideas are presented in a scattered form and in a barren and trite style, we cannot help being surprised by the success of Ibn Tūmart among his compatriots, and we are convinced that an extraordinary force of persuasion must have emanated from him when he spoke. His eloquence was indeed capable of moving the simple-minded Berbers. Moreover, he is presented as an eloquent orator by the chroniclers who say that he was equally eloquent in Arabic and in Berber.

However, his force of persuasion did not come exclusively from an effective eloquence and a rigid doctrine not displeasing to the Berbers. His opposition to the Almoravids was an important element in his success. He considered them as anthropomorphists, that is, according to Muslim theologians they were guilty of the greatest sin that man may commit, and he openly advocated rebellion against them. It seems evident that the Mahdī's religious doctrine found a ready response in the rough and rigorous Berbers', but his call to revolt against the Almoravids was certainly his most effective weapon among the Maṣmūḍa. At the very beginning at least, it appears that the inhabitants of the Atlas echoed Ibn Tūmart's call be-

[31] Even in the Orient, he was considered a *khārijī*. See on that point the article of F. Gabrielī, "Le origini del movimento almohad in una fonte storica d'Oriente," *Arabica*, III (1956), 1-7.

cause it had a political aspect and was hostile to central authority which had always been resented by the Berbers.

One can also assume that some ethnical antagonism separated the Maṣmūḍa from the Ṣanhāja or that, according to a tradition as old as mankind, the Almohad mountaineers were full of contempt coupled with envy toward the people of the flat country, including the former Saharans.

Ibn Tūmart not only preached a doctrine, but he also tried to organize a new community in and around Tinmel—and therein lies the originality and strong appeal of the Almohad movement. One of his great difficulties was the fact that Berber society in the High Atlas was cut up into very small fragments, separated from each other by ancient and stubborn rivalries. The Mahdī, who knew Berber society admirably well, used two methods to achieve the unity of which he dreamt: he kept the traditional social structure, without which nothing could be done, but he was able to institute a strict hierarchy, between the various strata in that society because of his infallible authority as Mahdī. Through this practice he intended to appease traditional rivalries. In addition, he instituted along with that ethnical hierarchy, a sort of technical hierarchy, with the purpose of compelling cooperation among individuals coming from different tribes and who, until that time, would not have worked together.

The issue of the Almohad hierarchy has been carefully studied by some Western scholars and rightly so, since it may be considered a sort of keystone of the Almohad reform movement and is probably the true stroke of genius which Ibn Tūmart displayed.

Instead of being satisfied with the personal influence he had been able to win as infallible Mahdī, he also succeeded in setting up in his small Berber society what may be called new institutions. They survived him and they were still viable when 'Abd al-Mū'min seized power.

Unfortunately this question has not been completely clarified, even after such detailed investigations into the problem as those of Ambrosio Huici Miranda[82] and J.F.P. Hopkins.[83] As a matter of fact, the three most ancient authors who mention Ibn Tūmart's hierarchy—namely, the *Kitāb al-Ansāb*,[84] Ibn al-Qaṭṭān,[85] and al-Marrākushī[86]—present contradictory evidence which is generally not very clear. It seems, however, that between Ibn Tūmart's period and the end of 'Abd al-Mū'min's reign profound transformations were brought about in the system; we surmise this rather than learn it from documents. It is therefore not easy to give an exact or adequate picture of the reorganization efforts of Ibn Tūmart, but one cannot deny the final result.

One thing is agreed on by everyone, that the Mahdī divided the Almohads into categories different from the traditional tribal groups. This does not mean that he suppressed the tribes, because such an attempt would probably have proved fruitless at that time. He seems

[82] *Op.cit.*, I, pp. 100-05.

[83] J.F.P. Hopkins, *Medieval Muslim Governments in Barbary* (London, 1958), chapter dedicated to "The Almohade Hierarchy."

[84] *Documents inédits*, pp. 29, 32-48/42-44, 48-73.

[85] Lévi-Provençal, *Six fragments inédits, op.cit.*, II, pp. 340-43/361-65.

[86] Al-Marrākushī, *History, op.cit.*, pp. 135-36, 247-49/163-65, 292-94. Other sources on the Almohad organization merely reproduce one or the other of these documents.

rather to have tried to reduce the influence of the tribal groups by superposing upon them other organizational forms which conformed in some ways with Berber patterns and which therefore had a chance of being accepted and allowed to take root. The Council of the Fifty is the best proof of this: an assembly was set up which was composed of some fifty members, representing what could be called the founder tribes of the Almohad movement, in other words, those who supported the Mahdī soon after he settled in Tinmel. Two groups were entitled to have more representatives than the others, the Hargha tribe, from which the Mahdī originated and in which he had launched his movement, and also the "Tinmel people" who welcomed him when he took refuge among them. It is to be noted that the "Tinmel people" did not include only autochthonous families but a great number of aliens who had associated themselves with the movement. Such a council is consistent with the Berber tradition of the *Ait Arbaʿīn* [the sons of the Forty] in regard to its size, its political role, and its proportional representation of various elements, but it greatly transcended the usual framework of the Berber assemblies because it united elements frequently opposed to each other in the past as well as bringing "foreigners" in residence at Tinmel into the movement or others designated as such by Ibn al-Qaṭṭān.[37]

In addition, two other organizations were set up which had no relation to the traditional institutions of the Maṣmūḍa: the "household people" [*ahl al-dār*], a sort of privy council which functioned in conjunction with the royal house; and the "Ten," that is, the original followers of

[37] *Op.cit.*, pp. 342/365.

the Mahdī who joined him during his stay in the Maghrib before he settled at Igīllīz. According to tradition, it is established that the "Ten" were the first men who had acknowledged him as the Mahdī and that among them were the prominent men of the movement, in particular 'Abd al-Mū'min, Abū Ḥafṣ 'Umar Intī, and al-Bashīr al-Wansharīsi.

If it is true that we are relatively well informed about those three groups so that we are able to see with sufficient clarity what they actually represented, we are also adequately informed about the order of precedence of the tribes for inspection and probably for battle, but we must recognize that we do not know much more than the names of the other elements of the Almohad hierarchy —the *muḥtasib-s*, or *mizwar-s*, the *ghuzāt*, "people of the *ḥizb*," etc. Mr. Hopkins has studied with the greatest care the various statements concerning them which have come down to us and he has tried to elucidate what they actually concealed, but he has not always succeeded, as he himself recognizes, because the information available is too vague or conflicting to permit any assurance about the place of these groups in the hierarchy.

It may be said, however, that military preoccupations played a large part in the elaboration of Ibn Tūmart's guiding principles, as was thoroughly emphasized by Robert Montagne:[38] the military connotations of the words *ghuzāt*, *ṭabbāla*, *rumāt*, and *jund* make this clear.

Furthermore, Ibn Tūmart decided personally to educate further a group of young men chosen for their unusual abilities and their previous intellectual pursuits—*ṭālib-s* and *ḥāfiẓ-s*, the words used for them, clarify their status

[38] Montagne, *Les Berbères et le Makhzen, op. cit.*, p. 63.

in the movement. The Almohad Official Letters, frequently directed to the shaykhs and *ṭālib-s* of a city or region, demonstrate that those men were considered very important by 'Abd al-Mū'min. One passage of *al-Ḥulal al-mawshiyya*[39] shows us 'Abd al-Mū'min organizing the *ḥāfiẓ-s*, 3,000 of them, into a sort of high officials' school or administration school, according to a pattern probably unknown at the time.

However obscure the details of the organization formed by Ibn Tūmart remain, it is certain that in his reorganization he attempted to reduce the influence of the traditional tribal framework, if not to break it up altogether. He certainly did not conceive of the enormous developments that were to take place in the Almohad empire later on, and, indeed, his hierarchy is not adapted to so wide a political entity but only to a group of Berber tribes of the High Atlas. Nevertheless, it is probable that later developments were greatly facilitated by his original reorganization because it made possible collaboration among tribes which would never have come together under the previous system.

In Tinmel, the Mahdī and his friends devoted their time to spreading the doctrine, organizing Almohad society, and fighting against the Almoravids. It was not always easy to spread the doctrine, notwithstanding the good will of most of the Berbers—these mountaineers were quite illiterate people and were accustomed to solving unaided the difficulties of their hard lives and practicing a very simple religion which was full of ancient

[39] *Al-Ḥulal al-mawshiyya, op.cit.*, p. 125; French translation by Lévi-Provençal, *Documents inédits*, p. 72,n3; Spanish translation by Huici Miranda, *Colección, op.cit.*, I, p. 180.

superstitions. They were ill-prepared to understand the Mahdī's message; their minds were generally unamenable to abstract ideas and furthermore they did not know a word of Arabic. Ibn Tūmart and his disciples were therefore obliged to use the Berber language in preaching.

The Mahdī was also obliged to resort to purely mechanical methods to inculcate some elements of doctrine in the minds of the humblest of the Almohads: for instance he obliged the people of Tinmel, on pain of punishment, to recite every day a new text of the Koran.

The facts presented on that issue, however, must be examined very carefully because nearly all of them originate from decided enemies of the Almohads, such as the Oriental historian Ibn al-Aṯīr, or the author of the *Rawḍ al-Qirṭās*, an unconditional supporter of the Marinides and therefore unfavorable to the Almohads.

It seems that Ibn Tūmart was obliged to take into account the nature of his audience, and therefore to use means far removed from the usual methods of the theologians and the cultivated elite. It would also seem that he put in use, without knowing it, what we would now call mass-communication procedures. Thus he is pictured[40] requiring each individual in a group of Berbers to learn first one or two words of a Koranic sentence, as if it were his own name. These individuals were then placed according to the order of the words in the sentence and asked to give their supposed names in sequence, so that, at the end all had heard the sentence in its right order and, since it was repeated several days in succession, came to know it by heart. Thus, little by little, using mnemonic procedures of that sort, adapted to the capabilities of the

[40] *Rawḍ al-Qirṭās*, *op.cit.*, pp. 118-19/160.

Berber mountaineers, he instilled in them a rudimentary knowledge completely unknown to them before his movement.

Men like Ibn al-Aṯīr or Ibn Abī-Zar‘ may ridicule such methods and see in them only coarse swindles, but in the eyes of twentieth century intellectuals who cannot ignore mass communication problems, the approach used by Ibn Tūmart seems wise and efficient. One may even say that on this point, as on many others, Ibn Tūmart appears as a true innovator.

His adversaries charged him with quackery; he may sometimes have used tricks for making an impression upon the simple-minded Berbers, but they seem to have been only a pious fraud. I do not accept the idea that Ibn Tūmart was an impostor who was activated only by ambition.

As a matter of fact, even his adversaries acknowledge that his life was completely austere and that he never tried to establish a dynasty: not only did he never marry nor have any children, but he did not put his relatives in high posts. His sister Zainab[41] was certainly one of his most influential confidants, but no available evidence shows that she took the least advantage of her position to further her own interests or those of her husband and son. As for his brothers, ‘Abd al-‘Azīz and ‘Isā, they were members of Ibn Tūmart's household, nothing more. If later on they thought they had a role to play and rebelled twice against ‘Abd al-Mū'min,[42] it was on their own initiative: no chronicler states that Ibn Tūmart had promised them anything. Therefore it is impossible to discover

[41] On her, see *Documents inédits*, pp. 30/44, 81/131.

[42] See Chapter II.

in the Mahdī's actions anything which indicates that he was a personally ambitious man. Certainly he wished to lead the Almohad community toward his high ideal and, in reaching that goal it was necessary for him to firmly establish his personal authority. In my opinion, this attitude derives from the fact that he definitely considered himself chosen by God to accomplish this mission. Briefly, I think he was convinced that he was an instrument of Providence and willingly accepted his pious mission, to which he devoted all the resources of his mind, including a natural astuteness that cannot be denied.

The superimposition of a new social organization upon the previous one did not always take place without difficulty; for instance, some tribes refused to accept the new order and the Mahdī undertook to force them into the movement. Some of the battles which were waged are described by the chroniclers, especially by al-Baiḏaq[43] and Ibn al-Qaṭṭān,[44] and it may be assumed that there were others. Ibn Tūmart, who was not only an idealist but also a skillful tactician, tried to win over his opponents in small groups; it is probable, therefore, that petty actions against villages or small groups within tribes, which are not mentioned by the chroniclers, were the most numerous actions taken. In any case, one may certainly think in terms of military conquest in the mountainous area around Tinmel. This campaign was brought to a successful conclusion during the life of the Mahdī with the help of friendly tribes—a victory won, not over the Almoravids who had no troops or strongholds in the

[43] *Documents inédits*, pp. 76-77/124.

[44] *Mélanges René Basset*, II, pp. 348-49/376.

Atlas range, but over the Berbers who opposed Ibn Tūmart's authority.

Even with the aid of friendly tribes the task of the Mahdī was never easy nor was his mission ever brought to a final victory because the savage individualism of the mountain people perpetually challenged his authority. Nearly all the chroniclers, favorable or not to the Mahdī, are in agreement that at the end of his life in the winter of 1129-1130, he decided to remedy once and for all the continuous instability among the tribes by making a serious purge. He entrusted al-Bashīr al-Wansharīsī, one of his first and most faithful companions, with the task.[45] The operation is called sorting out (*tamyīz*) by all the chroniclers and included two principles: a reorganization or confirmation of the order of battle of the Almohad tribes; and a bloody extermination of a great number of opponents or people lukewarm to the cause.

The following account by al-Baiḏaq[46] is probably an understatement of the real situation. It will be noted that the author does not give any description of the victims, perhaps because there were too many of them and he hesitated to provide the details of the mass killing—actions which had certainly not been made known by the Mahdī: "Many days went on and Allah provided the Mahdī with al-Bashīr's advice. Then he ordered the sorting out (*tamyīz*) of the party. Al-Bashīr undertook to exclude from the Almohads all those who were dissidents, hypocrites, and cheats, so that the treacherous were separated from the good. Then people saw the truth with their own eyes and the faithful redoubled their faith. . . . The

[45] On this purge, see *Documents inédits*, pp. 35-37/53-55, 53,n2.
[46] *Ibid.*, pp. 78/126.

sorting out in the party done by al-Bashīr lasted from Thursday to the Friday forty days after. People of five tribes were killed during that period. . . ." Then the author gives the names of the tribes purged and of the places where these actions took place.

Combined with the Mahdī's personal prestige these authoritarian measures seem to have increased the cohesion of the Almohad community rather than endangering it.

The Mahdī himself obviously believed that his power had grown since in the spring of 1130 he decided to attack Marrakesh, the Almoravids' capital. Before that he had been satisfied with pushing back their attacks which never penetrated very far into the hostile Atlas Mountains. The reason for the lack of aggression on the part of the Almoravids lies in the very composition of their army, the bulk of which was cavalry. The Atlas valleys, often narrow and nearly always uneven, did not offer a favorable ground for the maneuvers of horsemen. The paths in the mountain could easily be obstructed in many places; even when open this allowed the horsemen to advance only at a slow pace and this exposed them to additional danger. Some attempts made to enter the mountains resulted in serious failures,[47] and consequently the Almoravids quickly gave up a method which did not pay and had on the contrary been very costly in lives and war material.

They then attempted to keep the approaches to the plain closed by building fortresses at the entrance of the main valleys of the Atlas Mountains to the north. The best known of them is the fortress at Tasghimūt and im-

[47] *Ibid.*, pp. 74-77/119-23.

portant ruins of this building still stand.[48] For psychological as well as practical reasons, Ibn Tūmart did not accept the indignity of being besieged in his mountains, since the trade between the mountaineers and the plain tribes was one of the main aspects of economic life in the mountains and could not be cut off for long. On the other hand, because of the opposition which still caused tribes to revolt against the Mahdī's leadership in the mountains and which had not been completely destroyed by al-Bashīr's purge, he probably felt obliged to do something, both to divert the tribes' attention to the outside, a well-known device in such circumstances, and to make his enemies certain that he was strong and daring enough to seize power from the Almoravids. He therefore sent a strong expeditionary force against Marrakesh. The Almohads may have been practically invulnerable in their mountains but they were not accustomed to fighting in the open. They did, however, win initial success at the edge of the mountains and, encouraged by this, they advanced toward Marrakesh and besieged it. Surprised, the Almoravids at first took refuge in their walled capital, limiting their efforts to resisting the Almohad penetration. A short time later however the Almoravid sovereign received reinforcements from various places in Morocco and he ordered them to attack. A decisive battle was fought under the walls of Marrakesh, in a place called

[48] The Tasghimūt has been studied by Henri Basset and Henri Terrasse in their "Sanctuaires et forteresses almohades," *Hespéris*, VII (1927), 157-71 and by Charles Allain and Jacques Meunié, "Recherches archéologiques au Tasghimout des Mesfioua," *Hespéris*, XXXVIII (1951), 381-405.

al-Buḥaira, probably on May 13, 1130.[49] The Almoravid horsemen were free to execute their movements, and it is possible that the Almohads were inferior in number. In any case, the result was a severe defeat of the Mahdī's partisans whose only resort was to make a hurried flight toward the Atlas, leaving on the field a great number of dead, among whom was al-Bashīr. 'Abd al-Mū'min and Abū Ḥafṣ 'Umar Intī suffered from wounds but succeeded in escaping.

The Mahdī remained calm when he was informed of this defeat and the Almohad community was not noticeably shaken by this terrible blow, which proves that Ibn Tūmart's influence was already very deep.

The Almohads, however, were about to undergo a much more arduous test: Ibn Tūmart fell ill and died some months after the battle of al-Buḥaira. The generally accepted date of his death is August 13 or 14, 1130. Moreover, it is generally admitted that the Mahdī died in such circumstances that only five people, among whom was 'Abd al-Mū'min, knew of his death for some time.[50] They decided to withhold the information and to behave as if the Mahdī, although ill and confined to bed, was completely lucid and continued to give orders and to lead the community. Two or three years would pass before his death was made public and 'Abd al-Mū'min designated his successor. It seems evident that the Almohad leaders were surprised by the sudden death of the Mahdī,

[49] On the battle of al-Buḥaira, see Huici Miranda, *Historia política, op.cit.*, 1, pp. 8-84 and Gaston Deverdun, *Marrakech des origines à nos jours*, 1 (Rabat, 1959), pp. 155-57.

[50] *Documents inédits*, pp. 81/131.

and they concealed the fact during the time necessary to establish his succession. Though this is an acceptable hypothesis, it is nevertheless strange that this unusual situation was allowed to continue so long. However, al-Baiḏaq is categorical; according to him, the Mahdī was "ill" for three years,[51] but neither Ibn al-Qaṭṭān, whose text, it is true, was altered, nor al-Marrākushī mention an interregnum—the question of its existence has little chance of being answered now.

In any case Ibn Tūmart left his work incomplete, perhaps even hardly begun, since he failed in his main purpose—he had not succeeded in taking over the Almoravid government. However, even though he had not been able to win this victory, he had forged the tool of victory. Instead of the tiny and anarchical tribes that had lived in the Atlas before his time, he left in that region a community of quite a new type, still young and frail, but strong enough to survive the disaster of the attack on Marrakesh and above all to continue in fact after the death of the founder. This Almohad community in 1130 was still a profoundly Berber one, because Ibn Tūmart had kept a number of purely Berber institutions, such as the government assemblies, and he had retained the custom of the prestige of each tribe, et cetera. The Tinmel community was not, however, merely a Berber group but something wider and different: it was a religious society, whose principle was unity and whose binding element was the tremendous talent and character of the Mahdī. Surely the strict and austere Islam preached by Ibn Tūmart had done much to unite the High Atlas Berbers; but one may wonder whether the Mahdī's ascendency

[51] *Ibid.*, pp. 81/132.

and energy were not even more influential in this outcome. We would like to have more precise, vivid, and concrete details on this extraordinary man: an ascetic, but not at all a mystic; an eloquent man, but not a formal orator; a sharp and precise man—fascinating to be sure, inflexible in his commands—but humane enough to inspire rough mountaineers.

At the time of Ibn Tūmart's "death," Almohad unity was not extensive; it was limited to some valleys and some tribes in the Atlas. But the seed was full of vigor and possibilities. Some years later it had grown so rapidly that the Almohad empire had spread over the whole of North Africa. Without the new community created at Tinmel by Ibn Tūmart, such a development would not have been possible.

Before analyzing the development of the Almohad empire, it is advisable to look back and try to understand what the Almohad community was like when its founder disappeared.

There is no doubt whatsoever that Ibn Tūmart's personality, character, talents, and sense of mission were of great moment in the birth of the movement. Too many modern historians disregard the role of individuals in the evolution of societies and take into account only mass actions or economic and social situations. No one today disputes that those elements must automatically be considered in the study of the past. It does not follow, however, that the influence of some individuals must be reduced to the role of a mere symbol. Ibn Tūmart's career seems to hold significant overtones in this respect.

It is true that when Ibn Tūmart appeared on the Moroccan stage some Berber tribes were not fully satisfied with the Almoravid regime, but it consisted chiefly of a vague state of malaise which, as far as we know, had never yet taken the form of open rebellion. Without Ibn Tūmart's influence one is inclined to feel that the situation would have lasted much longer because the weight of the Almoravid empire was not onerous enough to stir up violent reactions quickly. In 1120, the Almoravid empire enjoyed an untroubled life. It was Ibn Tūmart who suddenly gave an extraordinary strength to the latent anti-Almoravid feeling among the Maṣmūḍa. He attained his goal by arousing the tribes against their domination by Berbers belonging to an ethnic group different from theirs, and by showing them that from a religious point of view the Almoravid's position was weak—true believers must rise up against those wicked guides. He was able to create a powerful force by merging political reactions, ethnic prejudices, and by arousing religious feelings through his eloquence.

He added to that force a moral posture and condemned the luxury of the Almoravid masters, in contrast to the simple life of the Berber mountaineers, who as a result of their convictions as well as of their way of life were accustomed to severe austerity. He, and he alone, aroused and then crystallized many latent feelings and reactions among the High Atlas Berbers.

Yet it is not certain that Ibn Tūmart could have started so widespread a movement had he not had behind him the whole strength of Islam. Here we venture into nearly unknown country since we are in possession of very sparse information on the development and evolution of Islam among the Berber tribes.[52]

[52] On that subject, see the works of Alfred Bel: "Coup d'oeil sur

We know only that if most of them became converted in such a short time to the new religion, they understood it in their own way and tried more or less consciously to adjust it to their former way of life and beliefs. Nearly all of them followed for a while the Kharijite missionaries who seeped into the Maghrib in the first quarter of the eighth century, about the same time as the Arab conquerors. Under the influence of men whom we should like to know better, such as the prophet Ṣāliḥ in the Barghawāṭa tribe, this Islam, already heterodox in itself, became "Berberized," retaining a sacred book in the Berber language as well as daily prayers. To a greater extent than was the case in orthodox Islam, they observed fasts and abstained from certain foods, but their practices were different from those ordered by the Prophet Mohammad. We also know that in the tenth century a religion inspired by Islam, but different from it on many points, was preached by the prophet Ḥā-Mīm of the Ghumāra tribe.[53] It seems evident that other beliefs of this sort, though short-lived and not widespread, were born in the Maghrib. It may be added that if Islam, more or less distorted, spread widely among the Berber tribes, it was a superficial Islam and only its general principles were known to them. It succeeded only in masking ancient rites, customs, and beliefs, the origins of which we ignore and of which we are hardly aware because the orthodox chroniclers feel reluctant to mention them.

Even if the Berber version of Islam is considered as un-

---

l'Islam en Berbérie," *Revue de l'histoire des Religions* (Janvier-Février 1917); *La religion musulmane en Berbérie*, I (Paris, 1938).

[53] On that prophet, see *Encyclopedia of Islam*, II, p. 266.

orthodox, it left a deep impression on Berber society. It had awakened in them the belief in God, one and almighty, and the desire to fulfill His commands as well as possible. This explains the success of the Almoravids who at first presented themselves as religious reformers and champions of the true Islam. We cannot assert, through lack of information, that all of the Berbers adhered to the Ṣanhāja's reform, but we are sure that before Ibn Tūmart none of them rebelled against Almoravid Islam.

The real genius of the Mahdī was contained in his presenting himself with the Koran in his hand, in demonstrating with the prestige he had gained after his long and studious sojourn in the Orient, that the Almoravids had failed in their religious mission, had become anthropomorphists, and did not yet behave according to the Law. Then, little by little, entire Berber tribes of the Atlas Mountains agreed to follow Ibn Tūmart because he had been able to convince them of his divine mission.

Yet the doctrine he preached was austere and severe. I have already pointed out that he did not hesitate to chastise harshly those who did not behave well or even to exterminate whole groups because he considered them bad Muslims. However, Ibn Tūmart knew his compatriots very well and was aware of the fact that they did not enjoy having too much flexibility and would readily accept the principle that crimes against the faith must be punished severely because most of them desired to be good and rigorous Muslims. Ibn Tūmart saw that every possible means for being good Muslims were available to them no matter how difficult; it is possible that without Islam, he would have remained only a petty rebel chieftain devoid of any promise. He asserted himself because he knew how to stir up the great religious ideals to which Berber souls aspired.

He was also able to go beyond the traditional framework by attempting to create a new society founded on principles different from those of the ancestral Berber society, just as the Prophet had succeeded in establishing a community in Medina which was not based on blood ties and respect for custom but was united by ties of faith and respect for divine Law. In the end, Ibn Tūmart's attempt to create a viable, cohesive empire did not succeed, and the Berber traditions were restored; but when he died his failure was not clear and the Tinmel community displayed some original characteristics: the Mahdī had succeeded in amalgamating diverse tribal groups which otherwise would probably have continued to live separated from and even hostile to each other. Something had changed in the Berber mountains—Ibn Tūmart had definitely shaken existing structures.

Nevertheless unity even in Ibn Tūmart's time was not perfect. Many tribes had joined the Almohad movement under coercion, as al-Baiḏaq's account proves. They probably waited for a lapse of Almohad authority to allow them to secede and to return to their former way of life. There was no equality even among the dominating tribes, and the hierarchy described by the chroniclers makes it easy to deduce that some groups, the Hargha and Tinmel people for instance, had precedence over others who probably resented it. In brief, when the Mahdī disappeared, unity was still very uncertain and ready to disintegrate if a strong guide was not there to take control of the destinies of the Almohad community and the future of the movement.

CHAPTER TWO

BUILDING AN EMPIRE

IBN TŪMART was now dead and finding a replacement for a man with his strong personality was no easy task. It has been established that the decisions about his successor were made by a very few individuals at the time of the announcement of the Mahdī's death, and were published only when they felt certain that no difficulties would arise. Whether it was a few days, a few months, or a few years after the event, remains quite uncertain.

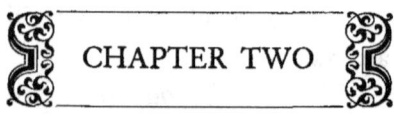

Ibn Tūmart's successor was one of his first disciples, 'Abd al-Mū'min ibn 'Alī whom he met at Mellāla when he was returning from Egypt. 'Abd al-Mū'min was accepted as Ibn Tūmart's successor though—or perhaps because—he was not a member of the Atlas tribes. Actually, he was a Berber who was born in the Trara range, a coastal range north of Tlemcen which is very far from Tinmel, and his tribe was definitely not of the same Berber clan as the Maṣmūḍa. It was perhaps less difficult for the Maṣmūḍa to accept an alien as their new leader than to accept any one of themselves who would necessarily have been a member of one of the local groups and for that reason probably unacceptable by the others. 'Abd al-Mū'min, one of the first and most cherished disciples, was about forty years old when the Mahdī died; on many occasions he had already given proof of his courage and his quick intelligence; his talents as a military chief and chief of state were to be proven in the future. He was recognized as caliph by the Almohad community in 1132 or 1133, or perhaps even as early as 1130.[1]

His beginnings were very modest; having learned the lesson of the disaster suffered near Marrakesh, he did not again attack the Almoravid forces on their own ground before he was sure he could overcome them. It is also probable that at this same time he was in secret contact with many tribes under Almoravid rule, spreading the political and religious ideas of the Almohads among them. Before bringing his troops into action, he thought it wiser to prepare the ground. We do not always have very precise details about military operations which took place, and the chroniclers do not say anything about 'Abd al-Mū'min's political actions during this long and obscure period, but they must have been skillful and efficient, since there was very little resistance against the Almohads' offensive, once it was launched.

After several years—seven or eight—of slow and patient preparations, after many minor campaigns, undertaken largely in the neighboring mountain regions and in the southern pre-Saharan zone,[2] 'Abd al-Mū'min left Tinmel in the spring of 1141; at that time he perhaps hoped but was not certain that he would never again reside in that tiny capital. Through an unfortunate lack of documentation it is impossible to know exactly what 'Abd al-Mū'min had in mind, but his whole conduct proves that beginning at this time, in accordance with the policy of the Mahdī, he began to drive the Almoravids out of Marrakesh and all their territories, largely because he considered them unworthy to lead a Muslim community.

[1] Al-Baiḏaq, *Documents inédits*, pp. 85/137.

[2] *Ibid.*, pp. 84-88/137-43.

There is also no doubt that he considered the Almohads as the only group capable of replacing the Almoravids, since they alone, in his opinion, could set the Muslims on the right path after they had been misled by the "anthropomorphist" Almoravids, and, since he was the chief of the Almohad community, he obviously considered himself the chief of the former Almoravid empire which should be returned to the "true" Islam.

Did he look farther? Did he dream during his obscure early days of domination over the whole Muslim West and of the establishment of his own family at the head of so far-flung an empire? No documentary evidence supports such a claim. We must therefore resign ourselves to almost complete ignorance concerning 'Abd al-Mū'min's motives—was he a clever opportunist who seized every opportunity as it presented itself or an ambitious man, fully conscious from the very beginning of his ultimate goal, who worked continuously to create opportunities which could lead him to that goal.

It is possible only to venture an hypothesis. As we take note of the zeal for reformation which was the primary motive of the Almohad movement, we may come to feel that 'Abd al-Mū'min at once conceived an idea of spreading the Mahdī's doctrine over all of North Africa and perhaps Spain. Had not Ibn Tūmart found fault with what he had seen in Tunis, Constantine, Bougie?[8] Therefore was it not desirable to have the Almohad reform triumph throughout these lands? Personal ambition aside —which may not be justified—'Abd al-Mū'min envisaged making his master's call known in the whole Maghrib, even when he was still in Tinmel.

[8] *Ibid.*, pp. 50-52/75-79.

It is not certain that he dreamt this early of establishing himself and his family at the head of an Almohad empire, although this notion cannot be completely discounted.

Proceeding slowly and methodically, he systematically avoided meeting the Almoravids in the open field, but established his authority over all of Morocco's mountain ranges one after the other: first, the High Atlas; then, the Middle Atlas; then, the Rif; and finally, the range south of Tlemcen.

Many scholars have emphasized this surprising game of hide and seek in which two adversaries used quite different weapons and were wary (through experience) of the dangers of taking risks in the other's territory. So 'Abd al-Mū'min, restrained by the bitter memories of the battle of al-Buḥaira, did not venture down into the plain, but worked his way through the mountains with great skill. At first glance these are startlingly unconventional tactics, but they were perfectly suited to the needs and military limitations of the Almohads.

For their part the Almoravid troops rarely left the plain. Most of the time they limited themselves to following the Almohad army, remaining within striking distance and waiting patiently for 'Abd al-Mū'min to enter imprudently an open field and expose himself to attack by the Almoravid cavalry. The Almoravids seem not to have understood that time worked against them, since they tried to block 'Abd al-Mū'min's advance with some weak columns that were always defeated. They did not have the daring needed to engage the Almohads in a decisive battle which was in all probability their only chance of crushing their enemy.

During his wanderings in the mountains, 'Abd al-Mū'-min did not limit himself to conquering territories but deliberately set about gaining adherents to the Almohad doctrine as well as recruiting warriors to his cause. And what warriors! Sturdy mountaineers, the ancestors of the twentieth century "goumiers," they could not be anything but excellent fighters. The account of al-Baiḏaq, who participated in the "seven years campaign," is explicit on this point: the Almohads were rarely opposed by the mountain tribes; on the contrary most of those tribes did not find it difficult to espouse the cause of the Almohads.[4]

Thus 'Abd al-Mū'min not only succeeded in practically cutting the Almoravid territory in two in the region of Taza and in developing around the Moroccan Almoravid region a kind of pincers movement in the Rif and Atlas ranges, but he also considerably strengthened his troops. Little by little he created an effective force, more and more comparable to that of his opponents. In the year 1145, in the region near Tlemcen 'Abd al-Mū'min finally decided he was strong enough to begin a decisive campaign in the plains between Tlemcen and Oran, and he won it. He then fell back on the plains of Morocco and proceeded to subdue first Fez and then Marrakesh after long and hard sieges—the latter in the spring of 1147.[5]

Marrakesh had been founded by the Almoravids and it was the very seat of their power: it is not surprising then that it put up a strong defense against the Almohads. Fez also resisted Almohad conquest at least as strongly as

[4] *Ibid.*, pp. 89-96/143-56.

[5] On the siege of Fez, see *ibid.*, pp. 99-102/162-67; on the siege of Marrakesh, see *ibid.*, pp. 102-04/168-71, and bibliographical notes by Evariste Lévi-Provençal in both cases.

Marrakesh; this makes it clear that many cities, if not all cities in the empire, had taken advantage of and enjoyed Almoravid prosperity, and for that reason they were strongly attached to the Almoravid cause. They dreaded the ascendancy of the Berber mountaineers who had a reputation of being austere primitives; they could not then see that these people were to build a more extensive, more civilized, and more prosperous empire than the Almoravids ever had succeeded in doing.

Once Fez and Marrakesh were conquered and the Almoravids vanquished, the Almohads were still not the masters of Morocco, for they had to face terrible revolts which imperiled their power.[6] The rebel moves took place in Southern Morocco (Sūs region) and on the Atlantic coast from Ceuta to Agadir; they were launched by at least two ringleaders who were seemingly devoid of any concerted plan and not in communication with each other. In spite of the lack of preparation for their rebellion, they were enthusiastically supported by the tribes, and were able to raise real armies of tens of thousands of men which on many occasions inflicted heavy defeats on the Almohad troops.

The rebels, hostile to the new power, were prompted by religious feelings. They rose up against the Almohad intransigence because the Almohads definitely condemned the Maliki school of law favored by the Almoravids. It has also been indicated[7] that the insurgent tribes were

[6] A very good study of those movements has been made by Ali Merad in his article " 'Abd al-Mu'min à la conquête de l'Afrique du Nord," *Annales de l'Institut d'Etudes Orientales de la Faculté des Lettres d'Alger*, xv (1957), pp. 122-31. The essential part of his documentation comes from the "Memoirs" of al-Baiḏaq.

[7] *Ibid.*

nearly all of them plains' tribes, and therefore they stood up firmly against the newly acquired power of the mountaineers. It is very likely that in many cases the antagonisms between unfamiliar and conflicting ways of tribal life played at least as important a role in their resistance as did religious differences. Summing up, one may say that the tribes of the plains resisted Almohad domination with great vigor while the mountain tribes submitted readily.

'Abd al-Mū'min faced the rebellion with his usual energy, and he succeeded in putting it down. He thought, however, that military victory was not enough, and he took advantage of an incident[8] (which the chroniclers do not describe clearly) to institute a purge of enormous dimension among the tribes which had just revolted and even among some of the Almohad tribes. If al-Baiḏaq is to be trusted, this operation called *i'tirāf* (recognition of the Almohad power) resulted in 32,780 deaths. Thus 'Abd al-Mū'min was led to take the most energetic measures in order to consolidate the victory of his movement in Morocco, and he did this with a cold intensity.

At about the same time, he was obliged to intervene in Spain where the decline of Almoravid power had provided the Spanish Christians with an opportunity for conquest. The Almohads, however, encountered fierce resistance from the Spanish population largely due to the unpopularity of the Berbers in Spain. People there remembered the demands made by Berber chiefs and troops at the time of the eleventh-century anarchy which had led to the fall of the Spanish caliphate. Then after 1086, the

[8] *Documents inédits*, pp. 109-12/181-85.

Almoravids had settled in Spain as the masters and they treated her as a conquered land. The Spaniards' aversion to the Berbers had increased greatly at that time.[9] When the Almohads, Berbers also, came to Spain even though they came as vindicators of the Islamic faith, the Spaniards stiffened their resistance. The rigidity of the Almohad doctrine was not at all in harmony with the intellectual and moral freedom which the Muslims of the peninsula were accustomed to enjoy.

'Abd al-Mū'min was therefore obliged to be content with occupying somehow the Occidental part of Muslim Spain because the provinces of Granada and Valencia did not accept his authority. It may be said, however, that, this region excepted, he had put under Almohad rule the entire Almoravid empire by 1150.

But he was not satisfied with that: in 1152 'Abd al-Mū'min launched a campaign against the Ḥammādid Kingdom of Bougie which he subdued without meeting much resistance. This Kingdom had been considerably weakened by the settling of Bedouin Arab tribes in the high plains of the Constantine area and it led a frugal life in and around its capital of Bougie. If the Almohads had an easy task in this connection, in contrast they had a difficult time subduing the Arab tribes.

According to al-Baiḏaq, the Almohads opened the battle with the Arabs,[10] which is not surprising. Having

[9] On the attitude of the Almoravid soldiers in Spain, see Evariste Lévi-Provençal, *Séville musulmane au début du XIIe siècle* (Paris, 1947), pp. 61-62.

[10] *Documents inédits*, pp. 114/189. It is stated here that after the caliph had reviewed the Almohads, "Yaslāsan ibn al-Mu'izz and 'Abd Allah ibn Wānūdīn, the caliph's son-in-law, went to fight the Arabs." The fact that we have no indication of the Arabs having

conquered Bougie, they considered themselves the heirs to the property of the former masters, that is, the whole province of Constantine. When they moved against the region of Sétif, they actually thought they were going into their own territory.

It seems that the Arabs reacted to the fall of Bougie without comment, but they saw no justification for their submitting to Almohad rule since they had never obeyed the Banū Ḥammād. When the Almohads seized upon the Qalʿa of the Banū Ḥammād, now Constantine, the Arabs formed a coalition that defeated the Almohads because, if we accept al-Baiḏaq,[11] of the rivalry which arose between the two Almohad chiefs who had been entrusted with the mission of fighting them. For three days they resisted fiercely the assault of the whole Almohad army which had launched an attack against them in the plain of Sétif.[12]

Some years later ʻAbd al-Mū'min answered a call for assistance from the Muslims of Ifrīqiya, who, seeing the Normans of Sicily occupying some of their harbors and gaining influence all over the country, asked the Almohads to intervene. He prepared his expedition with the utmost care and he brought with him a huge army; first he took Tunis, where he put an end to the Banū Khurāsān dynasty which had been reigning there for more than a century; then he laid siege to Mahdiya, the main

---

previously attacked the Almohads leads me to think that the initiative in the struggle was taken by ʻAbd al-Mū'min.

[11] *Ibid.* and H. R. Idris, *La Berbérie Orientale sous les Zirides* (Paris, 1962), I, pp. 365-74.

[12] Ibn Khaldūn, *Histoire des Berbères*, II, p. 190.

stronghold of the Christians, taking possession of it in January 1160.[13] The Normans were driven from Africa, and 'Abd al-Mū'min's power henceforth spread over Ifrīqiya and Tripolitania as well.

Thus, for the first time in North African history, as far as we know, that country was unified by the Berbers. Nobody would contest the fact that 'Abd al-Mū'min's personal qualities were a predominant factor in such an achievement. Equally as good a general as he was a political chief, he had been able to lead the Almohads to an unprecedented triumph. Yet he was right when he incessantly presented himself as the faithful heir of the Mahdī—'Abd al-Mū'min's achievement had been made possible by the enthusiasm that Ibn Tūmart had inspired in Maṣmūḍa's souls and through the organization he had been able to impose on the tribes.

'Abd al-Mū'min, however, was much less faithful to the Mahdī's teachings than he thought. True, he was very pious and always strictly observed the religious practices set up by Ibn Tūmart; but it is also true that he had neither the same eloquence, nor the same persuasive force, nor probably the same deep religious faith and knowledge as his master. We have some texts written by him on religious matters: all of them are tedious because there is nothing personal in them, nothing similar to the radiant faith of Ibn Tūmart. On religious ground, he seems to have retained only Ibn Tūmart's doctrinal severity and pietism. Thus when he had conquered Ifrīqiya, according to an oriental chronicler,[14] he gave the Jews and Chris-

[13] *Ibid.*, p. 193; Ibn al-Aṯīr, *Kamīl*, xi, pp. 160-62.

[14] Ibn al-Aṯīr, *Kamīl, op.cit.*, p. 159.

tians who lived there the choice between converting to Islam or death. According to all the evidence available, religious ceremonies and pious readings were then practiced at the court of ʻAbd al-Mūʼmin. One could not claim that he was careless of religious doctrine and practice as established by Ibn Tūmart: the Almohad empire under him was not less pious than the small community at Tinmel under the Mahdī, but that piety was more mechanical and official than it had previously been. A great military chief, a good administrator, an energetic and wise man, a sincere Muslim, but not one imbued with the passionate and radiant zeal of Ibn Tūmart, a man devoid of true religious qualifications—these words and phrases describe the basic characteristics of ʻAbd al-Mūʼmin.

Something else however, is apparent in him. Although he was the builder of the Almohad empire, he was also the first to implement its dissolution. Of course he did not endeavor to start undermining what he was building and was certainly persuaded that if he took the measures which he did, he would reinforce Almohad power; but actually he struck two blows from which the Almohad empire never completely recovered. Those two blows were delivered nearly simultaneously at the time of ʻAbd al-Mūʼmin's greatest power.

The first blow was the introduction into Morocco of some Arab Bedouin tribes. Up to that point the Arabs had not progressed beyond central Algeria in the region of Bū Saʼda where they had probably been stopped by the Almoravid empire. Once ʻAbd al-Mūʼmin had defeated and subdued them, he thought that he could utilize them for the holy war against the Christians in Spain, so he talked with them, trying to convince them that they should bring some of their tribes to Morocco in order to prepare them for Spain. This is always the reason given for his decision, but there was perhaps an additional reason for this decision.

There is no doubt that after the campaign of 1152-1153 against the Ḥammādid Kingdom, a grave crisis arose in the leading circles of the Almohads: two of the Mahdī's brothers who had survived him showed more or less open hostility toward 'Abd al-Mū'min, and they were joined in this by others. It is probable that the caliph felt that it would be useful to have at his disposal not only fighters for his holy war but also shock troops for his own defense, if necessary. This short-range calculation was sound from the short-range point of view, as we shall see in a moment, but at long range it appears to have been calamitous for the Almohad empire and dynasty. As soon as the caliph's authority tottered, the Arab tribes that had been settled in the very heart of the empire were in a position to intervene in general state policy. Since they had neither political ideas nor traditions, however, they sold their help to the highest bidder and became a force for anarchy and instability.

Some time later, in the spring of 1155, several Arab leaders requested 'Abd al-Mū'min to proclaim one of his sons as crown prince. Whether it was on their own initiative or whether they had been induced to make such a request is debatable. At first the caliph apparently refused but finally accepted, not too unwillingly, it seems. Then the Mahdī's two brothers rebelled openly and tried to seize power in Marrakesh, but they failed and were put to death. After this episode the Arabs again asked 'Abd al-Mū'min to appoint his sons as governors of the main provinces. Once more 'Abd al-Mū'min pretended to be surprised and refused, then he again changed his mind. The worst had happened: henceforth the empire was no longer solidly based on the Almohad movement, but had been converted to a hereditary empire for the benefit of the caliph's family.[15] Probably without understanding it clearly, 'Abd al-Mū'min had confiscated the empire on behalf of his descendants. Of course he and his successors continued to honor the Almohad leaders and to make a pretense of giving them a considerable role; actually, however, they were becoming more and more mere supernumeraries who were magnificently entertained. In consequence of such a deep change, the fruitful competition between the tribes on the one hand and religious zeal on the other (which the Mahdī had aroused) soon became blunted and disappeared completely; at the same time Berber particularism sprang to life, assuming that it had really been dormant. That development required a certain amount of time, but very soon it was quite obvious.

Thus, when 'Abd al-Mū'min died in 1163, the empire which he bequeathed to his successor was stronger in appearance than in reality, but it made a good superficial impression. Order was not always maintained without difficulty: in many regions it had to be maintained by force, but that was not surprising since the peoples of the

[15] For further details on those events, see Roger Le Tourneau, "Du mouvement almohade à la dynastie mu'minide: la révolte des frères d'Ibn Tūmart de 1153 a 1156," *Mélanges d'histoire et d' archéologie de l'Occident musulman*, II, pp. 111-16; Ali Merad, "Abd al-Mu'min," *op.cit.*, pp. 136-52.

Maghrib had not yet acquired the habit of living together; the part of Spain which was under Moslem rule had not been entirely subjected to Almohad power because in the Levante region, that of Valencia, Alicante, and Murcia, an anti-Berber movement had been started; 'Abd al-Mū'min was preparing an expedition to oppose the movement when he died.[16] Nevertheless the caliph's authority was more powerful and widespread than that of any Berber sovereign before him.

That authority was backed by an administration which, according to the information available, was certainly efficient and clearly demonstrated the capacity of 'Abd al-Mū'min as an administrator. Actually, as soon as he had completed the conquest of the whole Maghrib, he ordered that a general cadastral survey of all the land be made, separating cultivatable areas from forests and barren land so that taxes could be levied on a sound basis. We have unfortunately only a few lines written by a late chronicler of the fourteenth century about this land-tax organization which do not give any details by which an accurate assessment of the talents of 'Abd al-Mū'min and his collaborators and administrators could be made.[17] But in

[16] On the evolution in Spain, see Huici Miranda, *Historia política, op.cit.*, I, pp. 196-207.

[17] *Rawḍ al-Qirṭās*, pp. 129/174: "This year [1160], 'Abd al-Mū'min ordered the registration of land in Ifrīqiya and the Maghrib. The land from Barqa [Cyrenaica] to Wād Nūn in the Extreme Sūs was measured in leagues and miles in width and length. One-third of the registered land was composed of mountains, precipitous valleys, rivers, salt lakes, paths, and deserts, and the rest was subject to taxes. Every tribe had to pay its share in wheat and money. 'Abd al-Mū'min was the first to do so in the Maghrib."

any case, those few lines prove interesting and indicate that the caliph had some practical administrative ideas which were well adapted to his empire. What is also certain is that for a long time the Almohad financial situation was good and allowed them by and large to provide adequately for the needs of the empire. Again 'Abd al-Mū'min had retained Ibn Tūmart's institutions even if, from a general point of view, he had betrayed the Mahdī's spirit. Some of those institutions were even improved by the caliph: such as that of the *ḥāfiẓ* on which we are given the following information by an anonymous chronicler of the fourteenth century.

> He ordered that the *ḥāfiẓ* be taught the *Muwaṭṭa'* which is *The noblest book to be searched for*,[18] and other of the Mahdī's works. Every Friday after the prayer, he would summon them to the palace: the *ḥāfiẓ* gathered there, as many as 3,000, all of the same age, Maṣmūḍa and others. His aim was to educate them rapidly, according to his designs, so that one day he would have them riding horses; another day shooting with bows; then he would have them swimming in the pool of water that he had fitted up outside of his gardens: it was square and its perimeter measured about 700 yards; another time he had them rowing on dinghies and small boats which he had assembled there for them. They were educated in all those activities, receiving alternately rewards and punishments, and all their expenses and maintenance were paid for by the caliph

[18] The author is confusing the *Muwaṭṭa'*, a book of Mālik ibn Anas, the founder of the Maliki school of law, and the only known book of Ibn Tūmart.

> as were their horses and their weapons. When he had carried into effect what he had planned for them, he appointed them as governors of provinces and as senior officers in place of the Maṣmūḍa chiefs to whom he said: "The learned men come before you." The latter gave the management of affairs to the *ḥāfiẓ*, but 'Abd al-Mū'min had them remain beside the *ḥāfiẓ* in order to give them advice.[19]

In modern French the system described by the chronicler is an "école de cadres." 'Abd al-Mū'min saw to the training of new-style administrators for his immense empire, both learned in religious sciences and trained in different sports.

There is at last one point on which we are in a good position to appreciate 'Abd al-Mū'min's worth: he was fond of new buildings. At Marrakesh he built a palace of which unfortunately there is now no trace, and he also erected the fortress of Rabat on a rock dominating the mouth of the Bū Ragrag River—that fortress has been restored on many occasions and has not kept its primitive aspect.[20] He ordered mosques to be built at Taza,[21] at Tinmel,[22] and at Marrakesh—the famous Kutubiya mosque with a high, red, well-decorated tower.[23] Like his predecessors the Almoravids, he called upon the services of An-

[19] *Al-Ḥulal al-mawshiyya*, pp. 125-26; Spanish trans., pp. 179-80.

[20] Jacques Caillé, *La ville de Rabat jusqu'au protectorat français* (Paris, 1949), 1, pp. 83ff.

[21] Henri Terrasse, *La grande mosquée de Taza* (Paris, 1943).

[22] Henri Basset and Henri Terrasse, *Sanctuaires, op.cit.*, pp. 1-83; Henri Terrasse, *L'art hispano-mauresque des origines au XIIIe siècle* (Paris, 1932), pp. 284ff.

[23] Basset and Terrasse, *Sanctuaires, op.cit.*, pp. 84-273.

dalusian artists, but he gave them a new spirit: he substituted for the charming but perhaps exuberant decoration of the Almoravid period an austere and simple art that resulted in grandeur. The mosque of Tinmel in a narrow mountain valley is probably the most striking specimen of Almohad architecture. Only its ruins remain but they are important and have been preserved and restored in such a manner (by the specialized service of the French Protectorate), that it is possible to appreciate the majesty of its appearance before its decay. Having seen those monuments one may say that 'Abd al-Mū'min was not only the founder of a great military and political empire, the chief of an administration such as had never existed in North Africa, but also the creator or inspirer of a new architectural style—the most original and impressive in North Africa.

He had no taste for small details and he was not a sentimental person, as this anecdote quoted by the historian al-Marrākushī proves:[24]

> One day, one of his viziers was called into a magnificent garden where the caliph was sitting. Struck by the beauty of the place, he said some words of admiration and the caliph told him: "Is this what you call a magnificent scene?" Some days later the caliph reviewing his troops said to the same vizier: "This is a magnificent scene, and not your fruits and your trees."

If 'Abd al-Mū'min was denied a delicate taste, he had at least a sense of grandeur and may be counted among the most talented of the founders of Islamic civilization.

Behind this magnificent façade, however, serious faults

[24] *The History of the Almohads*, pp. 145/175-76.

lay in hiding—in the process of establishing his power 'Abd al-Mū'min had profoundly transformed the Almohad movement. He had not only abandoned the original principles of the movement for his family's profit, a move which was a complete contradiction of the Almohad tradition, but he had also for all practical purposes ceased to rely on the Maṣmūḍa.[25]

It is easy to believe that some of the Maṣmūḍa, understanding the situation very well, attempted to assassinate him in 1160 when he was on his way back to Marrakesh after the conquest of Mahdiya.[26] He was saved only by the self-sacrifice of one of his companions who, having got wind of the plot, informed the caliph and proposed to sleep in his tent in his place, thus offering to sacrifice his own life. The author of *Rawḍ al-Qirṭās*, who gives an account of this episode, states clearly that the plot had been hatched by some Almohads who were weary of the unceasing wars in which the caliph involved them.

Surely, we are justified in feeling that this was not the only reason for the assassination attempt. As a matter of fact, ever since the campaign against the Ḥammādid Kingdom 'Abd al-Mū'min had unceasingly followed a policy of magnanimity with the Arabs, and he tried to make them more and more attached to his person. It was obvious that with the exception of a few individuals like

[25] On that point, see the excellent observations of Ali Merad, "Abd al-Mū'min," *op.cit.*, pp. 153-60.

[26] Al Marrākushī, *op.cit.*, pp. 166/200-01; *Rawḍ al-Qirṭās, op.cit.*, pp. 130/175. The account of al-Marrākushī is not clear because he confuses this attempt to assassinate 'Abd al-Mū'min and the rebellion of the Mahdī's brothers. The account of *Rawḍ al-Qirṭās* seems to be sounder.

Abū Ḥafṣ 'Umar Intī, he did not at this time regard his first companions as his main support.

Some time after the attempt to kill him, he secretly sent word to the chiefs of his native tribe, the Kūmiya, asking for warriors to guarantee his security, "because he was an alien in the middle of the [Maṣmūḍa] tribes and had neither a family on which he could rely, nor a tribe on which he could trust or depend."[27] The Almohads were surprised by the arrival of so large a reinforcement[28] and wondered for a while whether the Kūmiya were coming as friends or as enemies. The caliph welcomed them in the best fashion and placed them in the second rank of the Almohad hierarchy, immediately following the Tinmel people, a decision which certainly offended most of the Almohads since the Kūmiya, as members of a different Berber group, were regarded as aliens.

It seems therefore that 'Abd al-Mū'min's intention was clear; since he understood that the Almohads were withdrawing more and more from him because he had seized power for his family, he relied on the Arabs and the Kūmiya, alien people who had not participated in the conquest of the Maghrib. In doing so, he made the Almohads more and more certain that 'Abd al-Mū'min's empire was no longer theirs, and this in turn gave his rule a fragile structure which was very different from the previous one.

The empire thus constituted lasted about fifty years: 'Abd al-Mū'min died in 1163, and the first signs of grave weakness in the Almohad state appeared with the severe

[27] *Rawḍ al-Qirṭās, op.cit.*, pp. 131/176.

[28] The number of 40,000 given by the chronicler is probably exaggerated.

defeat inflicted on the Almohads in 1212 at Las Navas de Tolosa in Spain by a Christian coalition which the Castilians led.

Between 1163 and 1212 three caliphs ruled successively: Abū Ya'qūb Yūsuf from 1163 to 1184; Abū Yūsuf Ya'qūb al-Manṣūr from 1184 to 1199; and Muḥammad al-Nāṣir from 1199 to 1213.

'Abd al-Mū'min's succession appeared to mark an important touchstone for the new dynasty. Were the Almohad shaykhs to struggle to revive the essential features of the Almohad movement in its primitive form or were they to abide by 'Abd al-Mū'min's desire to give his family absolute power among the Almohads? According to the chroniclers, the shaykhs did not interfere in the succession in any way. Being very wealthy they felt sure that the new caliph would respect their privileges, and they let 'Abd al-Mū'min's sons do what they wanted, including Abū Ḥafṣ 'Umar Intī. Abū Ḥafṣ' authority could have turned the tide: he was old and highly respected and his sons had been given good offices. Consequently, after some hesitation, he showed himself to be faithful to 'Abd al-Mū'min's family as he had been to the Mahdī. Yet it may be said that unconsciously he was less faithful to the spirit of the Almohad movement.

'Abd al-Mū'min's intentions, however, were not completely carried out. Earlier he had designated Muḥammad, his eldest son, as his heir, and, although the chroniclers' accounts differ considerably on the point, the Prince Muḥammad did retain power for some days or perhaps weeks. He was obliged, however, to give up his office because two of his younger brothers, sons of the same mother, formed a coalition against him: they were Abū

Ya'qūb Yūsuf who finally was proclaimed caliph; and Abū Ḥafṣ 'Umar, vizier under 'Abd al-Mū'min and therefore holder of extended powers.[29] The chroniclers of the Almohad epoch give very good reasons for such a substitution, and the fact that Prince Muḥammad gave up so easily is perhaps proof that he did not have either the energy or the character to become the master of so great an empire. Nevertheless the substitution was above all the result of a family intrigue in which the women of the family were probably involved. Obviously the reigning family was retreating farther and farther from the ideal of community life which Ibn Tūmart had tried to establish in Tinmel.

Furthermore Abū Ya'qūb Yūsuf's accession to power provoked some disturbance in the Mū'minid family: two of his brothers, the governor of Bougie and the governor of Cordova, stating that they were remaining faithful to the heir designated by 'Abd al-Mū'min, refused to swear allegiance to Abū Ya'qūb. Their opposition finally ceased after two years.

The caliph's brothers were not alone in threatening Almohad unity: some tribes of the Northern range of Morocco, the Ghumāra and others, rebelled, and the caliph was obliged to quell these rebellions with force. The inhabitants of the city of Gafsa in what is today Tunisia also rebelled at this time, but it seems the reasons for their uprising were purely local.

However, Abū Ya'qūb through skillful diplomacy as well as sheer force overcame all sorts of difficulties, and he was at length recognized as the caliph by everyone, prob-

[29] On the beginning of Abū Ya'qūb's reign, see Huici Miranda, *Historia política*, *op.cit.*, I, pp. 219-222.

ably in 1167. He then took the official title of Commander of the Faithful (*amīr al-mū'minīn*), when previously he had been satisfied with the title of prince (*amīr*).[30] As soon as he was assured of the throne, he behaved as his father had, bestowing many favors on the Almohad shaykhs but relegating the real authority to members of his family. It seems certain that, with him, possession of the Almohad movement was completely taken over by the Mū'minid dynasty—that is, it completely lost its soul. The consequences of this change were not yet obvious during Abū Ya'qūb's reign, in fact Almohad power increased under him and the caliph had a good share in that progress.

The new sovereign was a Berber. He was born in the High Atlas as both his father and mother had been and he had been very well educated. He spent a long time in Sevilla before his accession to the throne. While there he became fascinated by Spanish literature and art, and before his return to his native land he had acquired a sound Arab culture and developed a taste for books and architecture which resulted in Marrakesh becoming a center of intellectual life.

Abū Ya'qūb formed a personal friendship with the Spanish philosopher Ibn Ṭufayl, the author of *Kitāb al-Ḥayy ibn Yaqẓān* (the Book of the Living, Son of the Awakened),[31] and through Ibn Ṭufayl he came to know the great Ibn Rushd (Averroes) whose works he encour-

[30] One of his official letters (Evariste Lévi-Provençal, *Trent-sept lettres officielles almohades*, No. xxiv) begins with this, "From the amir Yūsuf, son of the Commander of the Faithful. . . ."

[31] *Hayy ben Yaqdhān, roman philosophique d'Ibn Thofaïl*, Léon Gauthier, ed. and trans. (2nd edn., Bayreuth, 1936).

aged.[32] On that point, he showed himself to be very different from his father who was primarily a man of action. Unquestionably the more sophisticated Almohad civilization really began to flourish during Abū Ya'qūb's reign.

All the chroniclers agree that after a few difficult years Abū Ya'qūb's reign was one of prosperity and peace. The sovereign organized imposing feasts in Marrakesh as well as in Sevilla and other places; taxes were collected without difficulty. Moreover, hardly sixty years after the Mahdī had founded in Tinmel a tiny community of mountaineers that was rich only in its people's energy, the Almohad empire had become an enormous political reality and it had acquired a satisfactory equilibrium.

Moreover Abū Ya'qūb not only received an immense heritage from his father, but he was able to increase it since he succeeded in subjecting to Almohad authority that part of Muslim Spain which had hitherto remained independent. In Spain he held out against many assaults by the Christians who showed themselves to be very enterprising. However, he generally remained on the defensive because he had not the same dynamism and military talents as his father. His expeditions against the Christian Spaniards were not always successful and the last, which was launched against the city of Santarem in 1184 ended in disaster and cost the caliph his life. The Spanish scholar Señor Ambrosio Huici Miranda, who made a very accurate study of those campaigns,[33] some-

[32] On the contacts of Abū Ya'qūb with Ibn Ṭufayl and Ibn Rushd, see G. Théry, "Conversations à Marrakech," *L'Islam et l'Occident*, in *Les Cahiers du Sud* (1947), pp. 73-91.

[33] *Op.cit.*, I, pp. 290-312.

times using unpublished documents, is extremely severe, and it seems rightly so, concerning Abū Ya'qūb's military ability. But even so, the Almohad empire was still very strong and solid when it was taken over by the deceased caliph's son, Abū Yūsuf Ya'qūb, who later took the honorific name of al-Manṣūr.

The chroniclers outdo each other in singing al-Manṣūr's praise, and they consider his reign the acme of Almohad power. A contemporary Moroccan writer, Muḥammad Rashīd Mulīn, devoted one of the very few historical books recently written in Arabic to *Political, Intellectual and Religious Life in Morocco under al-Manṣūr's Reign.* Actually, from many points of view, his fifteen-year reign was very brilliant.

The new caliph did not face the same difficulties as his father had when he ascended the throne: people were now accustomed to an hereditary succession and the Almohad shaykhs were as wealthy and amenable as ever. The army recognized him first, some days after his father's death, then the population of Sevilla. No member of his family rose against him, although he had not been proclaimed crown prince when his father was still alive. However, after a few years some of them did begin to arouse serious suspicions (1188); the assumption is that one of them was killed by a mob in Marrakesh, and two others were executed by order of the caliph.[34] In any case, this sort of thing is not unusual among Muslim dynasties in which princes of the blood are generally very numerous.

[34] *Ibid.*, pp. 338-40.

What is more serious is that almost immediately after he became caliph, Abū Yūsuf Ya'qūb was obliged to face a new sort of peril which gravely endangered his empire. When the Almoravid rule decayed, several members of an important branch of that dynasty, the Banū Ghāniya, took refuge in the Balearic Isles and organized there a small corsair state which they put under the lordship of the Abbasid caliph of Bagdad. 'Abd al-Mū'min was not master of eastern Spain, and he made no attempt to conquer it. After Abū Ya'qūb Yūsuf subdued that Spanish province, he entered into negotiations with the Banū Ghāniya, who agreed to give him a part of their spoils. He hoped that he would some day lead them to recognize his authority and worked in vain to incorporate them into his empire until he died.[35]

When information about the caliph's death (July 29, 1184) reached the island of Majorca, the new chief of the Banū Ghāniya, 'Alī, thought he saw his chance to create a new Almoravid state in North Africa. With some ships and a small army he disembarked at Bougie on November 13, 1184 and captured it by surprise; then he sent troops to Algiers, Miliana, Ashīr, and the Qal'a of the Banū Ḥammād which were conquered easily since there were very few Almohad soldiers in central North Africa—proof that the country had been quite calm. The Almohads launched a counteroffensive after some months, and recovered Bougie in May 1185, and the Banū Ghāniya were obliged to flee eastward.

Up to this point nothing extraordinary had occurred:

[35] On those events, see Alfred Bel, *Les Benou Ghâniya, derniers représentants de l'empire almoravide et leur lutte contre l'empire almohade* (Paris, 1903).

a bold raid had a happy ending owing to the element of surprise, but it was only a short-lived success because of the great disproportion of strength between the Banū Ghāniya and the Almohads.

However, 'Ali ibn Ghāniya had not remained idle on the African continent. He had obtained allies—some town dwellers, who had retained their loyalty to the dynasty of the Banū Ḥammād because they were of Ṣanhājan origin like the Banū Ghāniya, but of even greater importance, he rallied Arab tribes of the central Maghrib which barely tolerated Almohad authority.

In spite of their long subjugation, the Arab Bedouins had never become accustomed to the strict rule of the Almohads. Many of them therefore without hesitation took the first opportunity given them to throw off the yoke. Some Arab troops in the service of the Almohads went over to the enemy during the battle.[36] When Ibn Ghāniya fled eastward, whole Arab tribes of the central Maghrib followed him, and most of the Arab tribes of Ifrīqiya also supported him. As a consequence the Almohads were obliged not only to abandon a hopeless undertaking but also to quell a dangerous rebellion within their own empire. The alliance with the Arabs explains why the venture of the Banū Ghāniya lasted so long; it definitely ended in 1233, at a time when the entire Almohad empire was beginning to crumble.

Actually the Banū Ghāniya constituted only an excuse for rebellion against Almohad authority since the tribes of North Africa had in fact never accepted a system which proved to be altogether too severe and centralized. If the settled Berber tribes did not yet express their displeasure,

[36] Huici Miranda, *Colección, op.cit.*, II, p. 103.

migratory groups did balk, and not only the Arab tribes which openly sided with the Banū Ghāniya but also Berber groups, such as the Banū Marīn in the region of Figuig, remained outside of the Almohad system and refused to obey its laws. It is not an accident that the rebels' field of influence extended from Southern Tunisia and Tripolitania to the High Plains of today's Algeria: there, in the pastoral area, the Banū Ghāniya found not only tactical facilities but also the support of at least a part of the population.

After the first moment of surprise, Abū Yūsuf Ya'qūb reacted with vigor. He put himself at the head of a strong Almohad army and succeeded in inflicting a severe defeat on his enemies at al-Ḥamma near Gabès on October 14, 1187. After that victory he decided to settle in Morocco, close to the center of the empire and to several of the Arab tribes which had concluded an alliance with the Banū Ghāniya. His idea in doing this was to enable him to keep close contact with them and thus maintain his authority. He also planned to use them in his struggle against the Spanish Christians.[37]

As a matter of fact the Spanish Christians, encouraged by their victory against Abū Yūsuf Ya'qūb at Santarem and informed of the difficulties the Almohad caliph had to face in the Oriental part of his empire, launched more and more daring attacks against the Muslim territories in Spain.

As a result, when he thought he had finished with the Banū Ghāniya and their allies, Abū Yūsuf Ya'qūb led an important military expedition to Spain which culmi-

[37] G. Marçais, *Les Arabes en Berbérie du XIe au XIVe siècle* (Paris, 1913), pp. 198-202.

nated in the battle of Alarcos, west of Ciudad Real, on July 18, 1195. It was a great victory for the Muslims, as memorable as that of Yūsuf ibn Tāshfīn at Zallāqa in 1086, but it was a purely defensive victory without any territorial conquest. In the following years, the caliph conducted military expeditions in Christian territory around Toledo, Madrid, and as far as Guadalajara, but did not annex any of the immense territories he had traveled through. It must be observed, however, that on the occasion of the Alarcos campaign, the caliph, by proclaiming a holy war, succeeded in obtaining helpful assistance not only from the Almohad and Arab tribes but also from dissident Berbers, such as the Banū Marīn, and from previously rebellious tribes such as the Ghumāra. Therefore he could feel that despite the Banū Ghāniya's rebellion, the Maghrib was still strongly united with regard to the Christian enemy.

One might conclude from the foregoing that Abū Yūsuf Ya'qūb spent all of his reign in the field carrying out military operations which left him little time to pursue the arts of peace. Actually, such was not the case. Like his father he was a cultivated man and took a great interest in intellectual matters. If we except a rather short period of estrangement,[38] he patronized Averroes as his father had, and he frequently received the philosopher who died at his court in 1198.

But, above all, he built a considerable number of enormous buildings. In Marrakesh he created an entire city for his court and his administrative services:[39] it is now

[38] Huici Miranda, *Colección, op.cit.*, II, p. 200.

[39] Gaston Deverdun, *Marrakech des origines à 1912*, I, pp. 210-32.

known as Qasba. There he erected a great mosque based on a new concept[40] and had water brought to it.[41] He also built a hospital for the use of the population of Marrakesh.[42]

At Rabat where only a small fortress built by 'Abd al-Mū'min existed, Abū Yūsuf ordered the erection of an immense surrounding wall decorated with monumental gates; he probably intended to create a great city within these walls.[43] In any case he began to build a huge mosque, one of the largest in the whole Muslim world.[44] In Sevilla, he probably had the minaret of the Great Mosque completed, the famous Giralda, which his father had begun.[45]

We know many of those buildings: all of them offer the same majestic grandeur which is characteristic of Almohad architecture, but one may also perceive in them a tendency to the gigantic and the extraordinary—the Hassan mosque in Rabat, which was never completed, is visible testimony of this tendency with its unusual plan and its enormous proportions.

All this is magnificent and shows improvement over the previous reign, but it must also be acknowledged that some weaknesses are visible under the brilliant outward

40 *Ibid.*

41 *Rawḍ al-Qirṭās*, pp. 143/191.

42 Al-Marrākushī, *op.cit.*, pp. 209/249-50.

43 Henri Terrasse, *L'art hispano-mauresque* (Paris, 1932), pp. 288-290 and Jacques Caillé, *La ville de Rabat jusqu'au protectorat français* (Paris, 1949), I, pp. 125-149.

44 Jacques Caillé, *La mosquée de Hassan à Rabat* (2 vols., Paris, 1954).

45 Henri Terrasse, "*La grande mosquée almohade de Séville*," *Mémorial Henri Basset*, Paris, 1928, II, p. 253; *al-Ḥulal al-mawshiyya, op.cit.*, p. 132.

appearance. The first obvious flaw is the inability of Abū Yūsuf Ya'qūb to completely solve the problem of the Banū Ghāniya. To be sure he obliged them to seek refuge in remote countries where they could not do much harm, but there they remained and they were ready to take the first opportunity to strike again—they had never in fact been reabsorbed. On the other hand, it is under the reign of this philosopher-king that Almohad intolerance was at its highest point. The Jews, who officially had been converted to Islam but who were suspected of secretly practicing their own religion, were compelled to wear special and rather ridiculous clothes so that they were easily identified by the Moslems.[46] Moreover, the Mālikī school of law to which nearly all the Moslems in North Africa adhered, was completely banned, though it had hitherto been tolerated. To further aggravate the situation many works of the Mālikī school's leading authors were burned in the public squares, exactly as the Almoravids had done a century before to the best work of al-Ghazzālī.[47]

Moreover, according to nearly all of the chroniclers, al-Manṣūr had lost his faith in the Almohad doctrine: he considered the idea of the Mahdī's infallibility false and thought that the only guides for the Moslems were the Koran and the tradition of the Prophet.[48] Al-Manṣūr also understood, however, that Almohad tradition was one of the soundest pillars of the empire and this is probably the

[46] Zerkeshi, "Tarīkh al-dawlatain," *Chronique des Almohades et des Hafṣides*, Fagnan, trans. (Constantine, 1895), pp. 19-20; Al-Marrākushī, *op.cit.*, p. 223.

[47] Al-Marrākushī, *op.cit.*, pp. 201-02/241.

[48] *Ibid.*, pp. 212/253.

reason that he showed himself rigidly respectful of institutions whose essential validity he actually did not acknowledge. It seems likely that, at least a similar evolution was under way among the Almohad elite; many of the empire's leaders spent a part of their time in Spain, a country deeply imbued with secular ideas and which had never sincerely adopted Almohad doctrine. After such visits, they probably had a tendency to doubt, if not to reject, all that had constituted the true soul of the movement in the time of Ibn Tūmart.

Finally as the hold of the caliphal and of some other great Almohad families on the state became greater and greater, most of the tribes, Arab and Berber alike, had the feeling that they were in fact subjects under the control of an authority which was farther and farther removed from them. Those persons of influence who spent their lives in the palace at Marrakesh or in Spain were completely separated from the Berber masses over which they ruled. The exceptions were perhaps the first Almohad tribes that still enjoyed special consideration, according to the tradition of Ibn Tūmart which was even now respected; however, those tribes constituted a very small number in the empire. Consequently one has the impression of a power which remained very strong, but which was increasingly considered alien and tyrannical by most of the tribes.

Since the Banū Ghāniya encountered no difficulty in subsisting in North Africa all during al-Manṣūr's reign and long afterward, one may assume that they had benefited from the smouldering rancor.

The caliph may in the end have been under the illusion that he had subdued the Arabs once and for all by settling some of their tribes not far from his capital. As long as his central power remained strong, such an illusion was understandable. But the Arabs who had settled in the Atlantic plains of Morocco had not altered their previous behavior in any way. They were not really assimilated into the Moroccan population since their tribal groups, far from being destroyed, had been established in territories half depopulated by the wars at the beginning of ʿAbd al-Mū'min's reign. Therefore, they always constituted potential power which would be ready to assert itself as soon as circumstances would allow. Faithful to their particularist tendencies, the very presence of the Arabs introduced an additional source of agitation in Morocco which eventually resulted in anarchy. Moreover, they were to practice breeding, their century-old business, in an area where rewarding cultivation of the land was possible. Thus, the caliph had himself introduced into the heart of his empire a factor of political as well as of economic disorder. A late chronicler[49] asserts that he became conscious of his error just before his death and publicly regretted his decision. This fact is not certain but proves, in any case, that fourteenth-century Moroccans considered the presence of Arab tribes among them as a cause of disorder.

Although he was young—he was born in 1160 or 1161—Abū Yūsuf Yaʿqūb did not enjoy good health; he fell ill at the end of 1198 or the beginning of 1199 and, feeling he was at death's door, summoned his relatives, his principal officers, and his servants in order to give them his last recommendations.[50] He beseeched them to unite around his son and heir, to comply with God's precepts

[49] *Rawḍ al-Qirṭās*, pp. 152/201.

[50] Huici Miranda, *Colección, op.cit.*, II, pp. 206-12.

as expressed in the Koran and the Prophet's Tradition, to deal in a friendly way with the Arabs whom he had settled in Morocco, and to take care of "the orphans and the orphan-girl," that is, the Iberian Peninsula and its inhabitants. He died in his new palace at Marrakesh during the night of January 22 to 23, 1199.[51]

When al-Manṣūr died, the Almohad empire was still great, beautiful, and powerful. His son, however, was not able to hold sway over it: he should have been a very great man like his ancestors, but such was not the case. 'Abd al-Wāḥid al-Marrākushī, a chronicler who personally knew Muḥammad al-Nāṣir, the new caliph, gives the following description of him which is not as conventional as most of the similar portraits found in the Moroccan chronicles: "He had a clear complexion, a red beard, dark blue eyes, plump cheeks, average height; he often kept his eyes downcast and was very silent, mostly due to the faulty articulation from which he suffered; he was inscrutable, but at the same time mild, courageous, reluctant to shed blood, and not really disposed to undertake anything unless he had carefully studied it; he was charged with avarice."[52] Another chronicler, writing at a later date, adds this trait of character: "He was unable to bring his affairs to a successful conclusion without much work and managed his empire by himself, relying only on his personal feelings."[53] He was, in short, a timid, uncommunicative, probably authoritative sovereign, but without the brilliance which was largely responsible for the suc-

[51] Huici Miranda, *Historia política*, *op.cit.*, I, p. 385.

[52] Al-Marrākushī, *op.cit.*, p. 226.

[53] *Rawḍ al-Qirṭās*, pp. 158/202.

cess of his ancestors. Moreover Muḥammad al-Nāṣir was a very young man when he became caliph, since he was born in the spring of 1181,[54] and consequently he was more easily influenced by his environment and his chief collaborators. Perhaps the stress placed on the personality of the ruler may seem excessive when so many other powerful forces may by their very nature suffice to explain the fate of the Almohad empire. Although it is not my intention to minimize those forces, Almohad caliphs, after 'Abd al-Mū'min, enjoyed so much power that personality was of great importance, particularly at a time when the empire's solid institutions were still able to check the many centrifugal forces. It seems to me, therefore, that the personality of the new caliph (the first who lacked brilliance and influence) probably accelerated the evolution, and that is why I attach so much significance to it.

Naturally, the enemies of the Almohad empire tried to take every possible advantage of the change in rulers. Let us disregard here some rebellious movements in the traditionally restless regions of Sūs and the Ghumāra: these were quelled although not always very easily. In Ifrīqiya things were quite different: there, in addition to the Banū Ghāniya and the Arab tribes, a new rebel came to the front, Muḥammad b. 'Abd al-Karīm al-Ragrāgī, who, after having at first fought against the Arabs stood up against both the Almohads and the Banū Ghāniya. For a period he occupied Mahdiya and besieged Tunis, but he was killed by Yaḥya ibn Ghāniya in 1201 or 1202. Even if one regards his experience as accidental, it is at least a symptom of the great uneasiness which existed in Ifrīqiya.

[54] Al-Marrākushī, *op.cit.*, p. 225.

As a matter of fact, after having eliminated al-Ragrāgī, the Banū Ghāniya conquered Tunis and nearly the whole of Ifrīqiya during the year 1202.

At first al-Nāṣir's inadequate troops were routed by the rebels. It must be added that many Almohad chiefs showed themselves reluctant to engage the Banū Ghāniya in battle.[55] Finally, in 1204, the caliph organized a great expedition, as well-prepared as that of 'Abd al-Mū'min in 1159, and he started off toward the east in February 1205.[56] The operations were conducted, it seems, with great method, huge forces, and important war material. Tunis, abandoned by the enemies, was subdued without struggle; Mahdiya was besieged and the shaykh Abū Muḥammad 'Abd al-Wāḥid, son of the great Abū Ḥafṣ 'Umar Intī, decisively defeated the rebels not far from Gabès in October 1205, and Mahdiya surrendered in January 1206. Almohad authority was thus restored over Ifrīqiya.

The caliph had learned a lesson from the crisis; he understood that Yaḥya ibn Ghāniya had been beaten but not eliminated and could easily take advantage of the situation if another opportunity presented itself. Ifrīqiya was far from his capital so he decided that the region needed a special military and administrative setup in order to cope independently and quickly with any danger that might threaten it. He accordingly appointed as governor with extended powers the Hafsid, 'Abd al-Wāḥid, who had just displayed energy and ability.[57]

[55] Ibn Khaldūn, *Histoire des Berbères, op.cit.*, II, pp. 220-21.

[56] Huici Miranda, *Colección, op.cit.*, II, p. 229.

[57] Al-Tijānī (*Riḥla*, Tunis, 1958), pp. 360-62 and Ibn Khaldūn (*Histoire des Berbères, op.cit.*, II, p. 222) after him affirm that 'Abd al-Wāḥid required much pressing, accepted the office only for

Thus al-Nāṣir created on his own an autonomous province in his empire. For the time being he was right, since the threat of a Banū Ghāniya uprising remained present and 'Abd al-Wāḥid proved to be loyal to him. But what a temptation for an ambitious governor who had at his disposal a strong army, wide administrative powers, and strong financial resources! Actually the caliph, without being conscious of it, was preparing for the dismemberment of his empire which he now deemed too vast for him to govern singlehandedly.

While he was settling the Ifrīqiya affair, the Christian kings of Spain took advantage of his absence in order to attack Muslim territory—first the Aragonese king and then, after 1209, the king of Castile. Al-Nāṣir was therefore compelled to leave Marrakesh, where he had lived after his return from Ifrīqiya, in order to oppose the Christians' undertakings. Having proclaimed a holy war, he gathered a strong army in Ribāṭ al-Fatḥ, crossed the strait of Gibraltar in May 1211, and took the field soon afterward. During his march, serious deficiencies had appeared in the military administration of the Almohads: resupplying of the army had been completely inadequate. The caliph grew so angry at this defect that he had two high officials removed from office and later put them to death[58]—a serious indication of administrative failure and of unreasonable irritability on the part of al-Nāṣir.

---

three years and with almost entire freedom of action. The *Bayan*'s author (Huici Miranda, *Colección, op.cit.*, II, p. 241) does not note such requirements, but acknowledges that the new governor enjoyed extended powers.

[58] Huici Miranda, *Colección, op.cit.*, II, pp. 261-63.

The campaign began very well: at the beginning of September the Almohads seized the fortress of Salvatierra, but winter set in and military operations were suspended. When the summer months came, the Christian army moved against the Almohads; it was composed not only of Castilians but also of Aragonese and even of contingents from beyond the Pyrenees. The French soon gave up and the Spaniards alone moved against the Muslim army which was entrenched in the Sierra Morena and was keeping watch over the main passes. With the help of a shepherd, the Christians crossed the mountains through an unguarded pass which had been considered impassable and the battle was joined at Las Navas de Tolosa (*al-'Iqāb*) on July 16, 1212. Stubbornly fought at first, it was suddenly transformed and turned into a rout of the Muslims who fled or were slaughtered.[59]

The exaggerated figures given out by the Christians in order to magnify their victory must not be believed to the letter, but it is certain that the Muslim losses were extremely high. Nevertheless this victory does not contain the military implications often attributed to it, as Señor Huici Miranda has correctly pointed out.[60] The Almohad army in Spain was not annihilated and furthermore the Almohad armed forces in general were not involved. In addition, the Christians were unable to speed up conspicuously the reconquest of the Iberian Peninsula after their victory. It is important, however, not to underestimate the importance of the battle of Las Navas by going too far in

[59] On the battle of Las Navas de Tolosa, see Huici Miranda, *Las grandes batallas de la Reconquista* (Madrid, 1956), pp. 219-327.

[60] Huici Miranda, *Historia política, op.cit.*, II, pp. 428-29.

the opposite direction. It was the first great victory won by the Christians over the Muslims of Spain and Africa when they were led by their sovereign, and for this reason it took on symbolical value: it was not an Almohad army which had been defeated, but the Almohad empire with its caliph in command. At the time many thought that a reversal of fate was involved which until then had favored the Muslims.

From our point of view, the way in which the victory had been gained is much more significant. As soon as the Almohad army had been concentrated in Africa, deficiencies had appeared in the administrative organization. Then, the caliph's army, fighting against Christians who were spurred on by the desperation of the situation, had suddenly collapsed on the battlefield as if it had suddenly reached the end of its nervous energy and of its endurance. All or nearly all had fled, including the caliph. This was a sign that one of the essential springs of the Almohad machinery was broken: the bold and tenacious Berbers of Ibn Tūmart or 'Abd al-Mū'min persisted no longer. Their energy had been exhausted by their long dominion over an immense empire and they were beginning to show signs of weakness.

The Almohad leaders were perhaps themselves responsible for this Muslim defeat; they had become rich and wanted to enjoy their prosperity in peace; so they no longer had, as in the past, a taste for risk. In addition the soldiers had perhaps grown weary of their endless wars in Africa and Spain. To the Maṣmūḍa, who had formerly almost dominated the Almohad army, dissimilar groups had probably been added in great numbers—groups such as the more or less faithful Berber tribes, black troops, *ghuzz*, coming from the Orient, and Spaniards in the Iberian Peninsula. Thus the Almohad army was tremendous in numbers but heterogeneous and lacked cohesion. It is not possible to measure the share of each of these elements in the Almohads' military decline: the information we are able to gather, fragmentary and doubtful as it is, does not lead us to come to any firm conclusions. However, the defeat at Las Navas de Tolosa revealed beyond any doubt that the military organization of the Almohads was no longer what it had been at the time of 'Abd al-Mū'min and even of Ya'qūb al-Manṣūr.

It would be absurd to say that the battle brought about the ruin of the Almohad empire. That one failure was not devastating and the empire remained brilliant and solid for many years thereafter. Las Navas de Tolosa was only a symptom, the first important sign of the internal illness which was corroding the empire. More symptomatic perhaps was the fact that the defeat did not arouse any emotional reaction in the Muslim West. In earlier times such an event would have aroused the feeling that, Islam having suffered gravely at the hands of Spanish Christians, the Almohad state ought to avenge the Muslims for that defeat. On the contrary, after Las Navas de Tolosa, the Almohad empire seems to have been afflicted with a depressing passivity and dullness which reveal the moral situation among al-Naṣīr's subjects. Moreover, the caliph set the example: soon after the defeat, he came back to Marrakesh where he lived in idleness for a year until he died at the age of thirty-seven in late 1213. The chroniclers differ considerably about the circumstances of his death. Was he poisoned?[61] Was he accidentally

[61] *Rawḍ al-Qirṭās*, pp. 160/211.

killed by his Negro slaves?[62] Did he die after having been bitten by a dog?[63] Or did he have a stroke of apoplexy?[64] There is no good reason to accept one report in preference to another.

Thus for more than fifty years the Maṣmūḍas' empire, led by men of exceptional quality, had had a very highly developed civilization. This empire had received impetus from the Almohad reformation which caused it to flourish. There are periods when a human group is simply waiting for an impulse which suddenly activates its concealed energies, and it begins to develop a flourishing civilization. Ibn Tūmart had been able to provide that impulse, 'Abd al-Mū'min had known how to guide it, both being helped by Berbers of the mountains to whom they had been able to communicate their faith and who had shown many surprising qualities. Actually, it must be remembered, all of those men were Berbers; all or nearly all were born in the High Atlas Mountains, and furthermore this was the first time this situation had existed since the Moslem conquest. Hitherto Berber chiefs had been able to fight, sometimes successfully, against eastern invaders, or they had assisted a leader from the East to build a great kingdom: such had been the case of the two Idrīs in Morocco, of 'Abd al-Raḥmān ibn Rustum in Tāhart, and of the Fāṭimids in Ifrīqiya. However, the Zīrids in Ifrīqiya, the Banū Ḥammād in the central Maghrib, and the Almoravids in the Extreme West had shown

[62] *Ibn Khallikān, Wafayat al-a'yān*, IV, p. 346.

[63] Rawd al-mi'tār (Evariste Lévi-Provençal, *La péninsule ibérique au Moyen Age* (Leiden, 1938), pp. 138/166; Zarkashi, *Ta'rkh al-dawlatain*, Fagnan, trans., p. 24.

[64] Al-Marrākushī, *op.cit.*, p. 237.

that they were capable of founding strong states, but none of them had attained such magnitude and splendor as had the Almohads. Not only did the Almohad movement spread over the whole Maghrib and the Muslim part of Spain, but it had an extraordinary brilliance. Whether in architecture or in intellectual works, the Almohad empire bore very high the torch of Muslim civilization, which had declined steadily in the East since the end of the eleventh century. Indeed, there is no doubt about this: the Almohad empire was not only a political creation of unusual size, at least in the Occident, but also a new form of Muslim civilization which suddenly bloomed after centuries of slow maturing. Islam and the Arabs had their share in it, since the Muslim religion had given birth to the Almohad movement, and since the Arabic language and culture had been quickly adopted by the Almohad elite. But the Berbers also played an important part in that civilization: it was evident in the austerity, modesty, and I should also say, the crudeness that one finds in Almohad achievements. This crudeness was mitigated by the grace, moderation, and shrewdness of the Andalusian people. The uniting of all these different traditions and temperaments had made possible a combination of power, intellectual value, and taste for a certain form of beauty. And these, of course, are the main elements in a great civilization.

CHAPTER THREE

DECAY AND COLLAPSE

A CHIEF who would be able to restore it to its previous strength was a prime necessity for this empire that was beginning to falter. Unfortunately the fifth Almohad caliph, Yūsuf al-Mustanṣir, was not a strong or talented leader. He was recognized as a weak sovereign the very day of his father's death at the end of the year 1213. He was a young man of sixteen at most, perhaps only a boy of ten—our information is not sound on this point[1]—fond of pleasure (if we can trust certain chroniclers), who almost never left Marrakesh, probably because he did not have a very clear idea of his responsibilities and of the dangerous threats which were beginning to accumulate. All the chroniclers agree that his reign was peaceful, probably too peaceful, for if the new caliph had been of the same stamp as his ancestors, he would have left his palace more often and traveled through his empire—the foundations of which were crumbling and needed strengthening. The tranquility of the Almohad empire was not a good symptom at a time when the Christians were trying to consolidate their victory at Las Navas de Tolosa; when the Banū Ghāniya were always on the move; and when the Berber tribe of Banū Marīn, which

[1] Al-Marrākushī, Ibn Khaldūn, and Ibn Khallikān state that he was fifteen or sixteen years of age, but the others (*al-Bayān*, *al-Ḥulal al-mawshiyya*, and *al-Ḏakhirat al-saniyya*) say that he was only ten years old. For details, see Huici Miranda, *Colección*, *op.cit.*, II, p. 275n1.

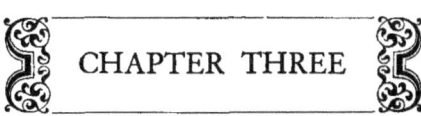

hitherto had remained quiet beyond the Saharan border of the empire, began to advance in the region of Taza and to inflict defeat on the Almohad troops which tried to push them back.

Actually al-Mustanṣir's reign is characterized by two series of events that show how deep a transformation the Almohad empire had already undergone. First, the caliph was much too young to govern by himself and therefore fell immediately under the influence of his viziers. If the members of the caliphal family enjoyed a real prestige among all the grandees and all the tribes, the viziers, whose power was essentially uncertain, were envied and frequently hated because they were members of a clan and had a general tendency to humiliate or eliminate their rivals of other clans. Moreover, we shall see that the viziers aspired to real power, and would not hesitate to dethrone the reigning caliph or to replace a dead caliph with one who was easy to control, that is, with children or well-chosen old men.

The second event is the appearance of the Banū Marīn.[2] They are a Berber pastoral tribe which, after the arrival of the Arab Bedouins in North Africa in the middle of the eleventh century had been obliged to leave their former lands in the region of Biskra and to settle in the high plains around Figuig. When the Almohads assumed power in North Africa, this tribe did not agree to live under their authority, and the Almohads sanctioned their taking up residence on the border of the desert. This proves *inter alia* that in the Central Maghrib, the Almo-

[2] On the beginnings of the Banū Marīn, see principally *al-Dakhirat al-saniyya*, Ben Cheneb, ed. (Algiers, 1921), and *Rawḍ al-Qirṭās*, pp. 184/240ff.

had empire did not extend beyond the coastal region called Tell. There on the border the Banū Marīn led an uneventful existence, grazing their cattle between the Figuig region and the middle valley of the Muluya River: an obscure tribe of medium size, very jealous of its freedom. On only one occasion were they willing to cooperate with the Almohads—when the caliph al-Manṣūr proclaimed a holy war against the infidels which resulted in the victory of Alarcos. Then the Banū Marīn sent him a contingent of warriors under the command of their supreme chief Maḥyū, who died of wounds received at Alarcos.

Now, suddenly the Banū Marīn, the year after the Muslim defeat by the Christians at Las Navas de Tolosa, appeared in the mountainous region along the coast, north of the Muluya River, with the obvious intention of settling in a province where Almohad authority had hitherto been undisputed. Was there some fact of which we have no knowledge that induced them to leave their accustomed grazing land—a drought perhaps? This is not impossible, although none of the chroniclers mention such an occurrence. It is also possible that, guided by their flair as sons of the desert, they felt that the Almohad empire was deeply shaken, and they were in a position to try their luck by settling on more favorable land. It seems that at the moment they had no political ambitions; they were merely seeking to improve their living conditions. In any case there is an amazing coincidence between the defeat of Las Navas de Tolosa and the appearance of the Banū Marīn in territories which they had never before been allowed to penetrate, and in which they had shown no interest.

Thus al-Mustanṣir's reign was not untroubled, and it clearly was during this period that the internal weaknesses of the Almohad empire became more serious and more deeply entrenched, though not immediately obvious. As it is said in the Holy Scripture: "Woe to the city whose prince is a child!"

Immediately after al-Mustanṣir's death in Marrakesh in 1224 (seemingly through some accident), the Almohad empire began to crack. The collapse of the Almohad power was complete by 1248 when the caliph al-Sa'īd died in the region of Tlemcen while trying to rebuild the empire of his ancestors. It is true that caliphs held some power in Marrakesh until 1269, and some Almohad authority remained in Tinmel until 1275, but these were mere "kinglets," heads of minute kingdoms that cannot be compared with the dominions of 'Abd al-Mū'min or Ya'qūb al-Manṣūr.

It is not useful to study this swift collapse in detail since the task has been carefully done by the Spanish scholar Ambrosio Huici Miranda.[8] This period of disintegration is similar to other periods of decay of a great power and is characterized by a great deal of confusion and by frequent unfortunate occurrences. Rather than give a detailed account of the facts, my purpose is to try to analyze how all this came about and by what mechanism North African unity was so quickly destroyed. To facilitate an understanding of the causes it is, however, advisable to present a brief summary of the events.

Immediately after al-Mustanṣir's death, an old man of

[8] Huici Miranda, *Historia política*, *op.cit.*, II, pp. 451ff; and "El reinado del califa almohade al-Rašid, hijo de al-Ma'mūn," *Hesperis*, XLI (1945), 9-45.

at least sixty and without any ambition, 'Abd al-Wāḥid, nicknamed al-Maslūkh (the dethroned), was brought to power by the Almohad shaykhs of Marrakesh who thought he would be a very flexible tool in their hands.[4] The motive behind that appointment is obvious: the great Almohad families were convinced that at last the time of the caliphal family had passed and that they would be able, after having suffered for more than eighty years under domination by 'Abd al-Mū'min and his descendants, to rule over the empire's destinies. At this time, however, the caliphal family was still popular among the masses and it was impossible to dethrone it. Fortunately the members of this family were numerous enough to make it possible to choose someone perfectly innocuous as ruler. The first leader chosen was an old man, and subsequent rulers were children.

But the Almohad shaykhs of Spain had not been consulted about the choice of the new caliph. One of them, who had been dismissed from favor at the instigation of one of the Marrakesh leaders, started a search for another caliph and found a readily available successor in the person of the governor of Murcia, al-'Ādil, who was a member of 'Abd al-Mū'min's family; he was actually a son of al-Manṣūr.[5] Of course the two caliphs could not agree, and a struggle between them and their troops ensued; the aim of the battle was the conquest of Marrakesh, the capital of the empire. In addition, a third candidate for caliph, 'Abd Allah al-Bayāsī, appeared in Spain where few troops were now stationed, and he tried to win the support of the Christian kings.[6]

[4] Huici Miranda, *Colección, op.cit.*, II, pp. 287-88.

[5] *Ibid.*, p. 289 and nl.

[6] *Ibid.*, p. 292.

In Marrakesh which he had conquered, the caliph al-'Ādil was soon assassinated, as his unfortunate elderly rival had been. Several tribes then rebelled, among them the Khulṭ, an Arab tribe. It was the first time that the Arabs had taken part in the struggle for power, but after that they were steadily and increasingly involved and played an important role in nearly all the following events.

Immediately after al-'Ādil's death, two new candidates declared themselves, one in Marrakesh, the other in Spain. The former was a young man of sixteen who was brought to power by the chief of Tinmel and of the Hintāta tribes—two of the most prominent Almohad personalities—in order to dominate the government since they believed they could do what they wanted with him. As a matter of fact, it seems that this caliph named Yaḥya had no other qualities than a stubborn perseverance in claiming his right to the throne. The other, Abū al-'Alā Idrīs, who took the caliphian name of al-Ma'mūn, was another son of al-Manṣūr and does not seem to have been lacking in character. He also wanted to be supported by the Christians of Spain and seems to have bought at a rather heavy price several hundred soldiers who were put at his disposition by the King of Castile: among other concessions, al-Ma'mūn pledged his word to allow the Christians to build a church in Marrakesh where they were to be permitted to follow their religion without restriction and even to ring bells—all contrary to Muslim usage.[7]

Is there a link between this policy of forced tolerance on a *quid-pro-quo* basis and a very important measure which was taken by the same caliph al-Ma'mūn? All the sources

[7] *Ibid.*, p. 313 and nl.

available agree that al-Ma'mūn abolished Almohad doctrine. A chronicler of the fourteenth century, whose very important work has recently been translated into Spanish by Señor Huici Miranda, reports that al-Ma'mūn expressed himself as follows in an official letter which, it is said, he wrote in his own hand for the doctors and officials of the empire: "You know that we have suppressed error and published truth, that there is no other Mahdī than Jesus, son of Mary, who alone has a right to the title of Mahdī. . . . This is the reason why we have abolished that Almohad innovation and have removed the word 'infallibility'. . . . Our lord al-Manṣūr had had the intention of announcing the fact of which he was much more aware than we, but he found no opportunity to do so." And the chroniclers add that, by his order, the name of the Mahdī Ibn Tūmart and consequently his title of "infallible," were suppressed in the Friday prayer and on the coins. At the same time some Berber words, which were still used in the Friday prayer, were also suppressed.[8]

Unfortunately the chroniclers do not give any information about the reasons that led al-Ma'mūn to take these extraordinary measures. Was he inspired by personal conviction, or by filial reverence, since he is said to have laid stress on the fact that his father had had the same idea, but had not found opportunity to publish it? Did he have, rather, a political aim, the desire to be considered as a new reformer and thus in a position to gather around himself all Almohad energies? Those documents available do not aid us in coming to a decision between these conflicting hypotheses, but what is certain is that the measure taken

[8] *Ibid.*, pp. 318-20; *al Ḥulal al-mawshiyya*, p. 137, Huici Miranda, Spanish trans., p. 192.

resulted in further aggravating the Almohad troubles. Disorder had been great during the five years following al-Mustanṣir's death. The Almohad structural framework, however, was still standing and could probably still have been consolidated because the essential principles of the movement remained the same, but after al-Ma'mūn's declaration the Almohad doctrine itself was partly repudiated. What then remained of the soul of the Almohad movement? Nothing, since it was precisely around the idea of the Mahdī and his infallibility that the Almohad movement had been constituted.

As I pointed out previously, 'Abd al-Mū'min had exploited the Almohad movement for the benefit of his family; in the time of al-Ma'mūn that family had become a sign of disunion, since many of its members were trying to wrest power from one another. With the family of 'Abd al-Mū'min split and the Ibn Tūmart myth destroyed, the Almohad community became a body without a soul, consisting of individuals or groups that had doubts and no longer knew which course to follow. One can easily imagine the attitude of many of the Almohads when they were informed of this surprising news. Many were scandalized and tried to hang on to the magnitude of the Almohad past and to the myth of Ibn Tūmart, as did Abū Zakariyā', the governor of Ifrīqiya and a descendant of the shaykh Abū Ḥafṣ 'Umar Intī, who retained in the Friday prayer the invocation to the Mahdī Ibn Tūmart, but suppressed the one for the current caliph.[9] Thus the decision taken by al-Ma'mūn was the immediate cause of a split in the Almohad empire. To be sure, it was not

[9] See R. Brunschvig, *La Berbérie orientale sous les Ḥafṣides des origines à la fin du XVe siècle*, I (Paris, 1940), p. 21.

yet a rupture: Abū Zakariyā' had only taken a measure of conservation, waiting to see what would happen. Nonetheless, Ifrīqiya was no longer in harmony with one part of the empire, which part we do not always know, since the two candidates for the caliphate were vying with each other for the city of Marrakesh, thereby making it difficult to ascertain where the official authority was. To the problem of political anarchy a great moral confusion was added for many people after al-Ma'mūn's declaration: it was as if they had lost any valid reason for trusting and hoping.

This unintentionally destructive reign lasted about four years, from 1228 to 1232. At a time when the situation was still very doubtful, when al-Ma'mūn had not yet been able to eliminate his rival and, on the contrary, had seen one of his own brothers rising against him in Ceuta, he died a natural death on his return from Ceuta where he had tried in vain to expel the rebel.[10]

He was replaced by his eldest son, al-Rashīd, a young boy of fourteen at most, who was brought to power by the joint efforts of his mother (a Christian slave) and some of the military chiefs. The young caliph's character was not yet formed and he merely followed the advice of his elders. However, he did immediately restore the Almohad doctrine. Unfortunately it was too late: the evil had been done, and Almohad moral strength was never again to be what it had been previously. Henceforth anarchy was widespread: nobody had confidence in the state. Individuals, and particularly the various ethnic groups, behaved according to their own immediate in-

[10] Huici Miranda, *Colección, op.cit.*, II, p. 338.

terests and no longer with a view to long-range general interests. Arab tribes were one group that behaved in this way, but in addition the Christian mercenaries, who had so long remained loyal to those who paid them, began to change sides abruptly, freely following their own interests: the mercenaries who served under al-Rashīd's rival suddenly deserted him, allowing the caliph to take possession of Sijilmāsa in 1233 almost without a struggle. This was at the time one of the main cities in the Saharan regions of Morocco.[11]

Moreover, the civil war began to ruin the economy; the most important cities, which were the main objectives of the battles, suffered excessively. Therefore, the citizens, who had hitherto been loyal to the Almohad regime largely because of the stability and security of the country, began to desert the Almohad cause. Finally, and this is the most serious fact, whole sections of the empire broke away. Spain, which was almost entirely under the control of Spanish Muslims, set itself free from Almohad authority. Soon after this the Spanish Christians took advantage of that situation and conquered important parts of the Muslim territory: Cordova fell into the hands of the King of Castile in 1236, and Valencia was conquered by the Aragonese King in 1238. In Africa itself the Ḥafṣid governor of Tunis, Abū Zakariyā', who had already taken a step toward independence under al-Ma'mūn's caliphate when he had ceased to mention the caliph's name in the Friday prayer, declared himself completely independent in 1236, making the Friday invocation in his own name preceded by the Mahdī's name; he obviously considered

[11] *Ibid.*, III, p. 68; "El reinado del califa almohade," *op.cit.*, p. 27.

himself the only true heir of the Almohad regime.[12] At the same time the Banū 'Abd al-Wād, a Berber tribe which had recognized 'Abd al-Mū'min's authority in 1145 and in return had received control of the province of Tlemcen, also proclaimed its independence under the command of its chief, Yaghmorāsan ibn Ziyyān.[13] As for the Banū Marīn, they now had political ambitions and levied taxes in the eastern part of Morocco, with the obvious intention of seizing every opportunity to extend their power to the Atlantic coast.

Although al-Rashīd and his followers were incessantly engaged in battle (some tribes and cities had already recognized his authority) and although his rival for the caliphate had been killed by an Arab tribe, nevertheless, when al-Rashīd died in 1242 of a chill he had caught during an outing, he left to his successor an empire torn to pieces. The new caliph, al-Sa'īd, was his younger brother, a violent but energetic mulatto. The beginnings of his caliphate were pitiful: revolts burst out everywhere and anarchy prevailed in those parts of the empire that remained. However, al-Sa'īd displayed an energy above the average and assigned to himself the task of recovering by force of arms the empire of his ancestors. He began by restoring his authority over Morocco, and obtained the submission of the Banū Marīn whose chief, Abū Yaḥyā, preferred to wait and see. Then, after having succeeded in

[12] R. Brunschvig, *loc.cit.*

[13] 'Abd al-Raḥmān Ibn Khaldūn, *Histoire des Berbères*, III, pp. 340-41; Yaḥyā Ibn Khaldūn, *Bighiāt al-Ruwad; Histoire des Beni 'Abd al-Wad*, Alfred Bel, ed. and trans., I (Algiers, 1904), pp. iii/147. Yaghmorāsan seized power in D̲ū 'l-qa'da in 633 (July 7 to August 5, 1236).

gathering a powerful army, he attacked the rebels of Tlemcen; he was, however, a victim of his own audacity, and he was killed in an ambush in the vicinity of Tlemcen in 1248.[14] In the same year the King of Castile conquered Sevilla, thus reducing Muslim territory in Spain to the narrow area of Malaga, Granada, and Almeria. Henceforth the Almohad empire was at an end: a caliph was extant in Marrakesh for more than twenty years, until 1269, but he exercised authority over only a narrow triangular area between the Umm al-Rabi' River, the High Atlas range, and the Atlantic Ocean. When the Banū Marīn conquered Marrakesh in 1269, an Almohad government settled in Tinmel and continued there till 1275. Thus the Almohads, stripped of their possessions, ended their regime in the narrow valley where they had begun under Ibn Tūmart. At one time they had ruled over the entire Muslim West. The fact remains that the Almohad empire was dead in 1248, after the failure of the caliph al-Sa'īd, and its complete collapse had taken less than twenty-five years.

Is it necessary to add that during the period of decay, Almohad civilization declined even more quickly than its political power? The only Almohad monument of that period—the walls of Fez, which had been destroyed by 'Abd al-Mū'min when he conquered the city and which the caliph al-Nāṣir ordered to be restored immediately after the defeat at Las Navas de Tolosa—holds special meaning for us. Such an enterprise is symptomatic of the state of mind in the empire in the year 1212: the caliph was apprehensive lest the Christian enemy bring the war

[14] Huici Miranda, *Colección, op.cit.*, II, pp. 193-94.

to the very heart of Morocco. Beyond that, nothing remains: palaces, mosques, philosophical books, even literary work disappeared from the scene. The Almohad historian al-Marrākushī alone continued to write after 1220, but for some unknown reason he lived in Egypt. In the Almohad empire itself, civilization was struck by impotence and stupor, and the wonderful artistic and literary flow of the second half of the twelfth century came to an abrupt end. The empire had neither time nor taste for thinking about anything except civil war.

We must now try to meditate on the true reasons for this collapse, which leads us to careful consideration and comparison of the general conditions of political life in North Africa, not only in the twelfth and thirteenth centuries but also in the twentieth century or contemporary period.

The first and most obvious explanation for the eventual failure of the Almohad empire is that it was too vast. At a time when means of communication were slow and difficult and in an area where the topography added special difficulties to those of distance, it was a gamble to attempt to maintain such a wide political community under a single authority. In addition, if Marrakesh was questionable as the capital of Morocco, because it was not centrally located even within that country, it was much too remote from North Africa as a whole, not to mention from Spain. The location of the capital was in fact one of the reasons why the caliph al-Nāṣir organized Ifrīqiya in 1207 as a quasi-autonomous province under the authority of a descendant of Abū Ḥafṣ 'Umar Intī.

Decay and Collapse

However, the challenge of maintaining the Almohad empire was carried out successfully for over half a century more, and that fact alone must give us a very high opinion of the Almohad administration. We do not know the administrative organization in detail, but we must appreciate its achievement at the time when the empire was at its apogee. The organization conceived by Ibn Tūmart at Tinmel and adapted by ʻAbd al-Mū'min to an immense empire proved itself and cannot be held responsible for the collapse, but it was obviously necessary that such a complex administration be directed by a very firm hand. When the caliph was an ordinary or mediocre man, it decayed. Obviously it may be assumed that the Almohad system was not bad in itself, but it had to function perfectly—at the first misfire of the engine, that is, of the caliph, the mechanism as a whole got out of order.

Only one important external cause of decay can be seen—the attacks of the Christian kingdoms in Spain. There, despite their enormous strength, the Almohads had been satisfied to repel Christian attacks, the great victory of Alarcos being a very good example of this plan: it was a defensive victory of which the caliph did not take advantage, whether he would not or could not is not clear from the evidence. Before that, his father had launched expeditions against Christian territories, but all of them had been failures, and the last one cost the caliph Abū Yaʻqūb his life. Thus the Almohads always had on their northern frontier—a very long frontier, the protection of which was very difficult—military and political powers which could do nothing against the empire when it was at its height but which were always ready to take advantage of the least lapse, as happened for example in

1212 at the battle of Las Navas de Tolosa, and which increased noticeably when Almohad anarchy left Muslim Spain to its own devices. It is possible to assume that Christian offensives produced only local results and had practically no influence on the internal situation of the empire, but I cannot make such an assumption. The Almohad movement was above all religious, having been created and advanced by a great religious enthusiasm. When Christian armies (which were according to contemporary sources the most hostile forces to be encountered in that part of the Islamic world) won victories over Muslim troops, it was a very hard blow to one of the mainsprings of the Almohad movement, the psychological one. Therefore it seems likely that defeat at Las Navas de Tolosa and the Christian victories of the year 1235 played an important role in the Almohad collapse through their strong psychological impact on the Muslim mind and mission. Of course, this was not the main reason: whatever their value and importance, the kings of Christian Spain would not have succeeded in destroying the Almohad empire if it had not suffered from serious internal disturbances. One may say, without great risk of error, that it destroyed itself.

It has frequently been assumed, particularly by Professor Henri Terrasse in his *Histoire du Maroc*,[15] that the Arab tribes played a great role in Almohad decay and that 'Abd al-Mū'min and al-Manṣūr had been mistaken in forcibly introducing the Arabs into Morocco, where they were in fact reluctant to come. It is true that those tribes contributed considerably to the disturbances in the year

[15] Henri Terrasse, *Histoire du Maroc* (Paris, 1949-50), I, pp. 360-61 and II, pp. 415-16.

1228 and the following years and that thereafter they greatly aggravated conditions which were approaching anarchy. The Arabs in Morocco were indeed aliens in that largely Berber country: consequently they felt free to do as they pleased when central authority slackened, and they denied themselves nothing. They were not restrained, as were most of the Berber tribes, by ancient alliances, ancient loyalties, and strong traditions. Brought to Morocco against their will, they considered themselves entitled to act according to their own immediate interests, which means that they made alliances with the highest bidder or with those that they thought offered them the best prospects for the near future, and they did not hesitate to reverse their position when circumstances justified.

After careful study it will appear that the Arabs only took advantage of circumstances which were not of their making. They were late in joining the game, at a time when several caliphs were already struggling for power and Almohad unity was already broken, so they cannot be held responsible for the Almohad decay: they only aggravated it when it was probably irremediable. In short, not unlike the Christian kings of Spain, the Arabs kept quiet as long as Almohad power remained strong; when it weakened, and only then, they entered the game. One cannot deny that in this period of Moroccan history, and later on during other periods of anarchy, they constituted a destructive influence but we must be careful not to exaggerate it. The Bedouin tribes only played that role when Morocco gave them the opportunity.

We must look elsewhere for the true explanation of the Almohad decline. I have already stated that I consider that 'Abd al-Mū'min bore the primary responsibility when he first sought to harness for the benefit of his family the wonderful élan through which the Almohads had conquered Morocco, Spain, and the whole Maghrib. But we must be precise in establishing his responsibility. When he set up an hereditary monarchy, in conformity with Muslim tradition (whether Umayyad, 'Abbāsid, or Fatimid), and when he entrusted to his sons and the members of his family the major responsibilities of power, 'Abd al-Mū'min destroyed the essential nature of the Almohad movement, which had consisted up to that time in the cooperation of the Berber tribes whose chief was recognized by them as enjoying religious power.

After 'Abd al-Mū'min and his descendants came to power, the ruler was no longer chosen for his religious qualities since his choice was decided by blood ties; he was no longer recognized by the tribes but rather by imperial dignitaries, among whom were the chiefs of the Arab tribes. Was 'Abd al-Mū'min, by this policy, conscious of destroying what Ibn Tūmart had patiently built up? I do not think so because, according to all the documents available, this man was not Machiavellian: he was energetic, brave, and frank. He acted as he did because he probably thought that he was, purely and simply, consolidating his master's work and at the same time securing the future of his own family—a normal, human act.

Furthermore, if we except the privileges granted to his family, the rest of the Mahdī's work remained unchanged: the tribal hierarchy conceived by Ibn Tūmart was maintained, and the different kinds of technicians were retained and sometimes their training was improved. Moreover the families of the first companions of the Mahdī, such as Abū Ḥafṣ 'Umar Intī, retained their privileges, the honors which had gradually been given to them, and their great responsibilities. Thus at the beginning of the thirteenth century, one of Abū Ḥafṣ' descendants was appointed governor of Ifrīqiya and was granted considerable power. Finally Almohad doctrine remained untouched: the writings of Ibn Tūmart were carefully studied, exactly as when the master was living, along with the Koran and the Prophet's tradition. Because so much time has now elapsed, we are able to ascertain that some changes were already taking place, but it seems that those then living were unaware of this fact (except the Mahdī's brothers, who in any case seem to have plotted against the regime for extremely personal reasons rather than for general and noble reasons).

However, by giving his family great powers, 'Abd al-Mū'min made possible the renunciation of basic Almohad doctrine by the caliph al-Ma'mūn, his great-grandson. It seems clear that al-Ma'mūn acted on his own decision in this repudiation. If he had followed the regulations set up by the Mahdī at Tinmel, he would have consulted his council on this momentous decision and there is every reason to believe that his council would have opposed the proposition and kept Ibn Tūmart's tradition. Proof of this statement is found in the fact that the Hafsid ruler of Tunis, proclaimed his attachment to the doctrine which was in fact the very basis of the Almohad movement and empire. Moreover, it appears clear that Abū Zakariyā', the ruler of Tunis, did not try to find a pretext for breaking with the Almohad caliph and for securing power for himself. On the contrary, he proceeded with great prudence, hoping, it seems, that wisdom would prevail and the Almohad tradition would soon be restored. One may therefore assert that the Mu'minid family, first through 'Abd al-Mū'min's actions and then through the behavior of al-Ma'mūn destroyed itself without being clearly conscious of it. They, in fact, deliberately did away with the very substance of the Almohad movement—sentimental attachment to a powerful doctrine—without which groups of men are like bodies without a soul. We find here one fundamental explanation not only for the Almohad collapse but also for the speed with which it occurred.

However, it seems to me that there are other reasons. I have emphatically insisted on the grandeur and beauty of the Almohad civilization, and I do not take back what I have said about it, but we must study it more closely and try to evaluate its influence. When we look at the walls and the mosques which were built by the Almohad caliphs, and when we read the philosophical works of Ibn Ṭūfayl or Averroes, we are right in admiring them, but we have a tendency to think that the whole empire participated in such magnificence, and this assumption is wrong. The Almohad civilization, as we see it, had been built up by a very small elite. It seems clear that it had been built up only by the sovereign and his court; all the great works whose beautiful remnants we admire were ordered by the caliph. The poets, the philosophers, the theologians, the historians, who after all were not many in number, were to be found only in the caliph's court at Marrakesh or around his governors at Fez, Sevilla, Tlemcen, or Tunis. Taking everything into account, this civilization was only a veneer, however brilliant it may have been, and beneath the surface there was quite a different reality.

Behind the façades of some of the cities which the

chroniclers describe in detail and which were neither very numerous nor well-populated, lived the masses of the Berber tribes and they were largely untouched by the Almohad adventure. Some of them, at the time of Ibn Tūmart, had been moved by an unquestionable religious zeal which had led them to the conquest of the empire, but this zeal soon became a pious habit, and lost its original vital force. Aside from this quickly extinguished zeal, the tribes had kept their generally miserable and primitive way of life, their ancestral mores (not always in conformity with Islamic teaching), and their Berber language. Because Arabic was used only among the Arab tribes, in the main cities, and in the court, the Berber tribes had practically no access to Arabic culture. Between that rural mass and the leading elite, there was nothing, since the middle class, existing only in some cities, was very small and in many cases was made up of people who had come from Spain, like Ibn Ṭūfayl, Averroes and the architects of the monuments built in Marrakesh or Rabat. It is probable that the sophisticated Andalusians showed nothing but contempt for the rough Berbers, and they did nothing to attract them to the brilliant civilization that they represented. I do not pretend to condemn the Almohad leaders and charge them with obscurantism. The modern attention to mass education was not a concern of that time; even if it had been, it would have taken a long time to spread the civilization of Marrakesh up to the High Atlas valleys, and the Almohad dynasty was to endure less than one century. The fact is nonetheless there: the Almohad elite accomplished great things, but they left behind an unchanged mass, and what is true about the tribes who participated in the movement at Tinmel is even more true about those peoples, Arabs included, who had been conquered and incorporated through pressure and violence into an empire for which they never showed any enthusiasm.

Here we are probably reaching the essential point. The Almohad empire, like the previous ones in North Africa, was an empire created by conquest. As the Berbers of the Western Sahara had established the Almoravid empire for their own benefit and without drawing the subdued populations under their administration into the government or cultural life, so the Almohad empire was founded by some Maṣmūḍa tribes of the High Atlas for their own benefit. The other populations of the empire were in the Maṣmūḍa's service. It is possible that the Maṣmūḍa, faithful to the teaching of the Mahdī and to his ideal of justice, used moderation and equity toward the vanquished; but in any case the relations were always those between victors and vanquished. The best proof of this is furnished by the Spanish Muslims who rebelled against Almohad domination as soon as it showed signs of weakness. Moreover, those Spanish Muslims had every reason to be prudent since they knew very well through long experience that the Christian enemy was lying in wait for them and they themselves were incapable of restraining the Christians. In spite of this recognition of their vulnerability, they did not behave prudently and anti-Almohad feeling having prevailed among them, they tried above all to get rid of the Berber conquerors. After all that, let come what may!

Another example of this same feeling is shown in the behavior of the inhabitants of al-Mahdiya in Ifrīqiya: they had called upon the Almohads in 1156 for help against the Normans of Sicily who had taken their city some years earlier, and they were liberated by 'Abd al-Mū'min. However, when an anti-Almohad rebel came to them in 1199, they welcomed him and sided with him after only forty years of Almohad domination. The Ghumāra tribe in northern Morocco also revolted many times because it had never accepted Maṣmūḍa authority.

I do not intend to condemn the Almohads or to charge against them alone an attitude which was in fact almost universally prevalent during this epoch. The fact, however, is there: the Maṣmūḍa ruled their empire as conquerors and failed to inculcate in other populations a sense of unity and security. The inhabitants of the big cities which directly profited from Almohad civilization and the peace it brought with it were in the end the only people who were faithful to the empire and never seriously opposed it, even in the final period of anarchy. I find this the main reason for the failure of the Almohads: the victorious Maṣmūḍa tribes who had been able to create an empire did not succeed in upholding it because they always kept the conquered population in a state of submission and never linked them into the administration of the empire.

I could stop there, but because of the importance of North Africa and the situation there at the present time, I feel inclined, having studied the Almohad experience, to reflect further on the general conditions of political life in North Africa. For some years many people, inside and outside North Africa, have spoken with enthusiasm of North African political unity. They seem, however, to ignore the fact that such a unity was once achieved in the days of the Almohad empire and that the final outcome of this unification was failure—and we have just examined the causes of this colossal failure.

The objection will be raised that general conditions are now not at all the same, and that what failed in the thirteenth century may now be successful. I agree in principle with such a statement, but I would like to present some reflections which may have some validity.

Neither geography nor history favors North African unity. Because of the topography and the climate, that country is divided into a rather large number of small regions, and the inhabitants are led by nature to live in quite different and sometimes conflicting ways. Division is sometimes carried to extremes, particularly in the mountainous regions where every valley actually forms a small country frequently separated from the next one by precipitous mountain slopes. And since, except in the relatively favored coastal regions, the climate itself makes human life difficult and unrewarding, the least-favored groups have always tried to find a new place to live at the expense of others.

The influence of this unfavorable environment have been many and compelling. They have in fact caused an historical evolution which we do not entirely understand due to lack of solid information, but what we do know allows us, I think, to understand better the age-old habits assumed by the inhabitants of this hostile land. They had an obvious tendency to constitute small political units, nearly always based until now on true or supposed blood ties; these units were traditionally and jealously closed to each other, the natives were suspicious of aliens, that is to say of neighbors, and frequently even hostile to them. It has happened occasionally that these units have successfully centered around a man or an idea, or, usually, around a man representing an idea. Such was the case when the tribes gathered around Kusaila and al-Kāhina to fight against the Muslim invaders, just as they had gathered around Jugurtha to fight the Roman invaders. On another occasion it was a preacher who attracted the Berber people: it was Maisara calling the tribes of Northern Morocco to revolt in the name of the Khārijite doctrine; or it was the missionary Abū 'Abd Allah who roused enthusiasm among the Kutāma when he announced the coming of the Mahdī; or it was Abū Yazīd who dragged behind him the mountaineers of the Aures, again in the name of the Khārijite doctrine; and finally, as we have seen, it was Ibn Tūmart who resumed the ideology of the Mahdī and made it take hold. In any case the determining factor which moved populations to unite was always the prospect of true justice. The Khārijite doctrine was the most leveling and uncompromising in the Islamic world, and the Mahdī was the man who "will fill the earth with justice and equity as it has been filled with tyranny and oppression." The idea which appealed to those populations who had a very hard life was not that of unity but that of a better, or at least of a less painful, life. It must also be noted that on every occasion when moves toward unity were made it was always one or another of the Berber groups that answered the call of the predestined man and followed him, since they were convinced that the better future envisaged was the future Berbers should enjoy and if the group succeeded in its purpose it would prevail for the sole benefit of the tribe. Universalism was absent in all those movements.

It will be noticed also that the Almohad movement

profited from particularly favorable circumstances: it was launched by Berbers for Berbers; no external interference, Muslim or otherwise, confused its development. It has been said that Christian influence in the Almohad collapse was weak and came too late to be of major importance. Nevertheless, the Almohad movement failed. North Africa never again found such an opportunity. At best, three states were formed within the territory of the old empire, and even these were not always cohesive.

One may claim that the past definitely dies and never returns, and that today's circumstances are so different from those of the thirteenth century that the Almohad failure is without meaning in the twentieth century. I agree with this statement, with this exception: although the past never returns, it does leave behind it very strong vestiges which take a long time to disappear. If individuals are in a large measure prisoners of their own past and of their ancestors' past, how much more so are groups of peoples? This is the reason that I cannot believe that a way of life which has lasted hundreds and probably thousands of years, will suddenly die out under the influence of new circumstances.

I do not mean that North African unity will never be realized, persuaded as I am that the country is now going through a more acute crisis than it ever has before. North Africa was suddenly put in contact with European civilization in the nineteenth and twentieth centuries; its native populations lived for decades in close touch with many dynamic European communities, and consequently a new and modern culture is now spreading over the country. All these factors are rapidly and deeply transforming North Africa to an extent difficult to measure exactly or to appreciate fully. Nevertheless, the old particularisms have obviously not yet died, and unity, if it is achieved some day in the future will bring many difficulties and probably much anguish. May such a unity, if it comes to pass, be less ephemeral than the Almohad unity!

A NOTE ON SOURCES

AND A LIST OF CONTEMPORARY ACCOUNTS AND HISTORICAL STUDIES

Some new sources of information may still be discovered on the Almohad era since the inventory of archives and libraries where they might be found, particularly in Morocco, is far from completed. Nevertheless, the sources of documentation on this period are now relatively satisfactory, and a list of contemporary accounts and modern studies is given on the following pages.

First among those sources which are contemporaneous with the events themselves, is a collection of Ibn Tūmart's works, *Kitāb a'azzu mā yuṭlab*, the compiling of which had been ordered by the caliph 'Abd al-Mū'min and which was published at the beginning of the twentieth century by J. D. Luciani. There are also the documents published, translated, and annotated with perfect accuracy by my late *maître* Evariste Lévi-Provençal: *Trente-sept lettres officielles almohades* and *Documents inédits d'histoire almohade* in which may be found some letters from Ibn Tūmart and 'Abd al-Mū'min, important fragments of a *Livre des généalogies* written in the first half of the thirteenth century and principally the *"Mémoires" d'al-Bayḏaq*, one of the first companions of the Mahdī Ibn Tūmart immediately following his return from the Orient.

To these may be added some chronicles written by contemporaries, of which only one has been published. They are: *al-Mu'jib* by 'Abd al-Wāḥid al-Marrākushī;

Naẓm al-jumān by Ibn al-Qaṭṭān, the first published fragment of which deals with the period between 500 and 1106 and 533 and 1138; and *al-Mann bi'l-imāma* by Ibn Sāḥib al-Ṣalāt of which only a fragment is known that deals with the period between 550/1155 and 578/1182.

Since this book was written, three important chronicles of the Almohad period have been published in Arabic. The first consisted of fragments of the book of Ibn al-Qaṭṭān, *Juz' min kitāb Naẓm al-jumān*, published by Doctor Mahmūd 'Alī Makkī, al Matba'a al-Mahdiyya (Tetuán, n.d.); the second is an important part of *al-Mann bi'l-imāma,* published by 'Abd al-Hādī al-Tāzī (Beirut, 1964); the third is the third part of Ibn 'Idārī's chronicle, *al Juz' al-tālit min kitāb al-Bayān al-Mughrib*, edited by Ambrosio Huici Miranda with the collaboration of Muhammad Ibn Ṭawīt and Muḥammad Ibrāhīm al Kittānī (Tetuán, 1963).

Then come the great chronicles generally known for some time: *Kāmil fi'l-ta'rīkh* of Ibn al-Aṯīr; *al-Bayān al-mughrib* of Ibn 'Idārī al-Marrākushī; *Rawḍ al-Qirṭās* written by a man whose name alone is known to us, Ibn Abī Zar' al-Fāsī; *Ta'rikh al-dawlatain* attributed to a writer named Zerkeshi; *al-Ḥulal al-mawshiyya*, an anonymous work of the fourteenth century; and *Kitāb al-'ibār* by Ibn Khaldūn.

The history of the Almohad period gave rise to a rather large number of studies, the principle ones are: The first history published was a superficial and not very scholarly study by a French diplomat, René Millet. Then come those studies undertaken by the brilliant team of the Institute of Higher Moroccan Studies, with Henri Basset, Henri Terrasse, Robert Montagne, and Evariste Lévi-Provençal.

There are also some chapters devoted to the Almohads in the well-known syntheses of Charles-André Julien, Emile-Félix Gautier, Georges Marçais, and Henri Terrasse. Finally, the thorough studies recently published by Ali Merad, J.F.P. Hopkins, and above all by the Valencian scholar Ambrosio Huici Miranda, to whom we are greatly indebted for a number of excellent translations, with annotations, and an important political history of the Almohad empire. We also now have the important contributions of Gaston Deverdun on Marrakesh, capital of the Almohad empire.

The work by Muslim scholars has been limited; besides the work of Merad, mentioned above, we have only a study in Arabic by the Moroccan, Muḥammad Rashīd Mulīn, on al-Manṣūr's epoch; another by Muḥammad Manūnī, also in Arabic, on the cultural life in the Almohad period; and a doctoral thesis in French by the Egyptian Sa'd Zaghlūl on the caliph al-Manṣūr. One may hope that young Moroccan scholars will soon contribute to the study of Almohad history in proportion to its importance in Moroccan history and the Muslim West.

As a matter of fact much is still to be done in the field. First of all, there is the hope that some unknown books or documents still lie hidden in the Moroccan archives and libraries. It is therefore necessary to continue as soon as possible with research and the inventory of the collections of documents which still remain unexplored.

Since Señor Huici Miranda has limited himself to the political study of the Almohad movement, the need still remains to draw a picture of the economic and social life of the Almohads, as well as of their intellectual evolution.

Sources

Notwithstanding the studies which have been devoted to the matter, more than one problem remains: for example, the chronology of Ibn Tūmart's life and death, the hierarchy which he instituted and 'Abd al-Mū'min modified, the administrative organization of the Almohad empire (and the reasons why it collapsed so rapidly) have not received satisfactory treatment.

To sum up, this epoch, so attractive from many points of view, still merits further study.

I. Contemporary Accounts

Le livre de Mohammed ibn Toumert, mahdi des Almohades, with an introduction by I. Goldziher. Algiers, 1903.

Trente-sept lettres officielles almohades, Arabic text edited by Evariste Lévi-Provençal. Rabat, 1941.

Evariste Lévi-Provençal, "Un recueil de lettres officielles almohades; étude diplomatique, analyse et commentaire historique," *Hespéris*, XXVIII (1941), 1-80, and as an offprint, Paris, 1962.

Evariste Lévi-Provençal, *Documents inédits d'histoire almohade, fragments manuscrits du "legajo" 1919 du fonds arabe de l'Escurial*, text and translation, Paris, 1928.

'Abd al-Wāḥid al Marrākushī, *The History of the Almohades*, Arabic text edited by R. Dozy. 2nd edn., Leiden, 1881.

E. Fagnan, trans., *Histoire des Almohades d'Abd el Wâhid Merrâkechi*. Algiers, 1893. New Arabic edition: *Al-mu'jib fi talkhīs akhbār al-Maghrib*. Cairo, 1949.

Ibn al-Aṯīr, *Kāmil fī 'l-ta'rīkh*, edited by C. J. Tornberg. 13 vols., Leiden, 1867-1874 (passages concerning the

Almohades are to be found in Vols. x to xii). Two French translations of this work have been made: E. Fagnan, *Annales du Maghreb et de l'Espagne*, Algiers, 1901; de Slane, *Ibn Khaldūn, Histoire des Berbères*, ii, Appendix v, pp. 573-93.

Ambrosio Huici Miranda, *Colección de crónicas arabes, de la reconquista*, ii and iii.

Ambrosio Huici Miranda, *Al-bayan al-mugrib fi iḫtiṣar ajbar muluk al-Andalus wa al-Magrib por Ibn 'Idārī al-Marrākusī*. Spanish trans., Tetuán, 1953-1954.

Ibn 'Iḏāri, *al-Juz' al-ṯāliṯ min kitāb al-Bayān al-Mughrib*. Arabic edition edited by Ambrosio Huici Miranda with the collaboration of Muhammad Ibn Ṭawīt and Muhammad Ibrāhīm al-Kittānī. Tetuán, 1963.

Abū'l-Ḥasan 'Alī ibn 'Abd Allah Ibn Abī Zar' al-Fāsī, *Annales regum Mauritaniae a condito Idrisarum imperio ad annum fugae 726*, edited and translated into Latin by C. J. Tornberg. 2 vols., Upsala, 1843-1846. French translation by A. Beaumier, Paris, 1860.

E. Fagnan, trans. *Chronique des Almohades et des Ḥafcides attribuée à Zerkechi*. Constantine, 1895.

Al-ḥulal al-mawshiyya, chronique anonyme des dynasties almoravide et almohade, edited by I. S. Allouche. Rabat, 1936. Spanish translation by Ambrosio Huici Miranda, *Colección de crónicas árabes de la reconquista*, I, Al-ḥulal al mawshiyya, Tetuán, 1952.

Ibn Saḥib al-Ṣalāt, *al-Mann bi'l-imāma*. Arabic edition by 'Abd al-Hādī al-Tāzī. Beirut, 1964.

Ibn al-Qattan, *Juz' min kitāb Naẓm al-jumān*. Arabic edition by Doctor Maḥmūd 'Alī Makkī, al-Matba'a al-Mahdiyya. Tetuán, n.d.

Sources

Ibn Khaldun, *Kitāb al-'Ibar.* Bulaq, 1867, vi, pp. 323-62. French translation by de Slane, *Histoire des Berbères,* ii, pp. 158-257.

II. Historical Studies

René Millet, *Les Almohades, histoire d'une dynastie berbére.* Paris, 1923.

Henri Basset, "Ibn Toumert, chef d'Etat," *Revue de l'histoire des religions,* ii (1925), 438-39. In collaboration with Henri Terrasse, *Sanctuaires et forteresses almohades,* Paris, 1932.

Henri Terrasse, *L'art hispano-mauresque des origines au XIIIe siècle,* Paris, 1932; *La mosquée des Andalous à Fès,* Paris, 1941; *La grande Mosquée de Taza,* Paris, 1944.

Robert Montagne, *Les Berbères et le Makhzen dans le Sud du Maroc.* Paris, 1930.

Evariste Lévi-Provençal, "Ibn Toumert et Abd al-Mūmin; le 'fakih du Sus'et le 'flambeau des Almohades,'" in *Mémorial Henri Basset,* ii, Paris, 1928, pp. 21-37.

Charles-André Julien, *Histoire de l'Afrique du Nord.* 2nd edn., ii, Paris, 1952, pp. 92-131 (revised by R. Le Tourneau).

Emile-Félix Gautier, *Le passé de l'Afrique du Nord: Les siècles obscurs.* Paris, 1937.

Georges Marçais, *La Berbérie musulmane et l'Orient au Moyen Age.* Paris, 1946, pp. 253-75.

Henri Terrasse, *Histoire du Maroc des origines à l'établissement du Protectorat français,* i, Casablanca, 1949, pp. 261-367.

Ali Merad, "'Abd al-Mu'min à la conquête de l'Afrique du Nord (1130-1163)," and "Contribution à l'histoire de la dynastie mu'minide (1163-1223)," in *Annales de l'Institut d'Etudes Orientales de la Faculté des Lettres d'Alger*, xv (1957), pp. 109-63 and xx (1962), pp. 401-75.

J.F.P. Hopkins, "The Almohade Hierarchy," in *Medieval Muslim Government in Barbary until the Sixth Century of the Hijra*. London, 1958, pp. 85-111.

Ambrosio Huici Miranda, *Historia pólitica del imperio almohade*, 2 vols., Tetuán, 1956-1959; "El reinado del califa almohade al-Rašid, hijo de al-Ma'mūn," *Hespéris*, XLI (1954), 9-45; "La leyenda y la historia en los origenes del imperio almohade," *Al-Andalus*, XIV (1949), 339-76.

Gaston Deverdun, *Marrakech des origines à 1912*. I, Rabat, 1959, pp. 151-301.

Muḥammad Rashīd Mulīn, *'Asr al-Manṣūr al-muwaḥḥidī*. Rabat, 1946.

Muḥammad Manūnī, *Al-'ulūm wa'l-adab wa'l-funūn 'ala 'ahd al-Muwaḥḥidīn*. Tetuán, 1950.

Sa'd Zaghlūl, *Abū Yusūf al-Manṣūr l'Almohade (1184 à 1199)*. A thesis defended at the Sorbonne in 1952. Unpublished.

INDEX

'Abbāsid dynasty, 4
'Abd al-'Azīz, 36
'Abd al-Mū'min ibn 'Alī, 16, 25, 31, 33, 36, 41, 48, 81, 92, 102; early years, 49-50; military tactics of, 51; and Almohad rebellion, 54; campaign against Ḥammādid Kingdom of Bougie, 55; religious faith of, 57-58; "confiscation" of Almohad empire by, 59-60; death, 60, 66-67; training system of, 63; as builder, 63-64; failure of, 105-107
'Abd al-Rahmān ibn Rustum, 87
'Abd al-Waḥid, Abū Muḥammad, 82
Abū al-'Alā Idrīs al-Ma'mūn, 94
Abū Bakr, 17
Abū Ḥafṣ 'Umar, son of 'Abd al-Mū'min, 68
Abū Hafṣ 'Umar Intī, 24, 27, 33, 41, 66-68, 96, 101
Abū Ya'qūb Yūsuf, 67, 69-71
Abū Yūsuf Ya'qūb al-Mansūr, 67, 71-72, 74, 79-80, 92
Abū Zakariyā', 96-97
al-'Ādil, 93-94
Ait Arba'īn (sons of the Forty), 32
Alarcos, battle of, 75
Alexandria, Egypt, 6
'Alī ibn Yūsuf, 23
Allain, Charles, 40n
Allouche, I. S., 8n
Almohad army, defeat of, 84-85
Almohad civilization, influence of, 107-108
Almohad community: characteristics of, 43-47; on death of Ibn Tūmart, 42; internal revolts in, 53, 73
Almohad doctrine, repudiation of, 96
Almohad empire: after battle of Las Navas, 86; Christian attacks on, 83, 98, 100, 102, 104, 109; decay and collapse of, 89-114; development of, 43-44; end of, 100; failure of as conquerors, 109-110; greatness of, 80, 107; intolerance of, 77; originality and strength of, 30; reasons for decline, 104-106; successive blows to, 58-59; tranquility of, 89
Almohad hierarchy: consolidation of power in, 54; elements of, 32; as keystone of movement, 30-31
Almohad movement: birth of, 3-47; religious nature of, 103, 105
Almohad Official Letters, 34
Almohad power, collapse of, 92, 104-106
Almoravid empire, 5; and attempts on life of Ibn Tūmart, 27; extent of, 11-12; growth of, 14; Ibn Tūmart's mission to overthrow, 6; his fighting against, 34; Marrakesh as seat of power, 52-53; Moslem law and, 24; Spanish influence in, 12
Arab conquest, in Maghrib, 11
Arabs, Moroccan, 79, 104
Atlas Mountains, 4, 24, 26, 34, 39, 44, 48, 51, 87, 108
Averroes (ibn-Rushd), 69-70, 75, 108

Index

Baidaq, al-, 10, 15-16, 19, 21-22, 37, 47, 52, 56
Balearic Isles, 72
Banū 'Abd al-Wād tribe, 98
Banū Ghāniya tribe, 72, 78, 81, 89; rebellion of, 73-75
Banū Ḥammad tribe, 72, 87
Banū Khurāsān dynasty, Tunis, 56
Banū Marīn tribe, 74-75, 89-90, 99
Barghawāṭa group, 13
Bashīr al-Wansharīsī, al-, 33, 38, 40
Basset, Henri, 28n
Bayāsī, 'Abd Allah al-, 93
Bedouin tribes, 11, 55, 90
Bel, Alfred, 72n
Berber language, 4
Berber tribes, North Africa, 3, 6, 13, 20, 25, 28-29, 34, 44, 54, 85; Almohad movement and, 11, 112-13; Arabic culture and, 108; dissatisfaction among, 13-14; mass-communication techniques used with, 35-36; unification of North Africa by, 57; unity of, 42-43
Berque, Jacques, 4n
Book of the Revival, 7
Bougie (Bijaya), Berber capital, 11, 15, 68, 72; fall of, 55-56; moral atmosphere of, 15-16
Brunschvig, R., 96n, 99n
Buḥaira, al-, battle of, 40-41, 51
Bū Ragrag River, 63

Caillé, Jacques, 63n
Christian kingdoms, attacks by, 83, 98, 100, 102, 104, 109
Constantine, province of, 56
Cordova, Spain, 5
Council of Fifty, 32
Council of Ten, 32-33

Dawūd, Abū, 18
Deverdun, Gaston, 75n

école de cadres, 63
"Extreme West" (Morocco), 6-7, 87-88

Fāsī, 'Allāl al-, 20
Fatimid caliphate, 12, 87
Fez, Morocco, 15, 22; conquest of, 52
Figuig, oasis of, 90-91
fuqahā' (doctors of the law), 14

Gabrielī, F., 29n
Garsīf, Morocco, 22
Gauthier, Léon, 69n
Ghazzālī, al- (Abū Hāmid Muhammad al-Ghazzālī), 6-7, 9, 14
Ghumāra tribe, 45
God, belief in, 46
Goldziher, I., 28n

ḥāfiẓ, organization of, 34, 62-63
Hā-Mīm, prophet, 45
al-Ḥamma, battle of, 74
Hammādid dynasty or kingdom, Bougie, 11-12, 55, 59
Hargha tribe, 3, 26, 47
Hopkins, J.F.B., 31, 33
Ḥulal al-mawshiyya, al-, 6, 34

ibn 'Abd al-'Azīz, 'Abd Allah, 20
ibn 'Abd al-Halīm, 'Abd-al-Ṣamad, 20-21
Ibn Abī-Zar', 36
Ibn al-Atīr, 5n, 6, 35-36
Ibn al Qaṭṭān, 31-32, 37, 42
ibn Ghāniya, 'Ali, 73
ibn Idrīs, Idrīs, 5
ibn Khaldūn, 19-20, 56n, 82n
Ibn Rushd (Averroes), 69-70, 75, 108
Ibn Sāhib al-Salāt, 6
Ibn Taizamt, 23
Ibn Ṭūfayl, 69, 108

Index

Ibn Tūmart (Muhammad ibn 'Abd Allah Ibn Tūmart), 3; ancestry of, 4; birth, 5; religious reform mission of, 6; mission to overthrow Almoravid dynasty, 8; early convictions about religious reform, 10; Berber "call" to, 10-11; preaches in Bougie, 15; meeting with 'Abd al-Mū'min, 16-18; teaches law, 20; arrives in Marrakesh, 22-23; concept of Moslem law, 24; proselytizing of, 25; proclaimed Mahdi, 25; veneration from Berbers, 26; scheming mind, 26-27; religious reform, 6, 26-27; escapes Almoravid army, 27; founds new community and fortress in Tinmel, 27-28; doctrine of, 28-29; infallibility of, 29; persuasive force of, 29; and Almohad hierarchy, 30-33, 54, 105; military aspects of, 33; organizing ability of, 34; mass-communication techniques of, 35; attack on Marrakesh, 39; defeat at battle of al-Buḥaira, 41; death, 41; successor to, 48; religious doctrine of, 58; "myth" of, 95-96; tradition of, 106
ibn 'Umar, Abū Bakr, 13
Ibn Wānūdīn, 'Abd Allah, 55n
Ibn Wuhaib, 23
ibn Yāsīn, 'Abd Allah, 12
Idris, H. R., 56n
Ifrīqiya, Moslems of, 3, 56, 81, 87
Igīllīz-n-Hargha, 3
Islam (religion), 4, 28, 88; evolution of in Berber tribes, 44-45; forced conversions to, 57-58; rites and customs of, 45-46
i'tirāf, 54

Jews: forced conversions of, 57-58; intolerance toward, 77

Kharijite missionaries, 45
Kitāb al-Ansāb, 31
Kitāb al-Hayy ibn Yaqẓān (Ibn Tūfayl), 69
Kitāb Ihya 'Ulūm al-Dīn (al-Ghazzālī), 7
Koran, 10, 14, 18, 28, 35
Kūmiya tribe, 66
Kutāma tribe, 12
Kutubiya mosque, Marrakesh, 63

Las Navas de Tolosa, battle of, 84-85, 89, 91, 100, 103
law: Maliki school of, 53; teaching of, 20, 46
Le Tourneau, Roger, 8n, 60n
Lévi-Provençal, Evariste, 3, 4n, 15n, 31n, 34n, 55n, 69n, 87n
Livre d'Ibn Tūmart, Le (Luciani), 28
Luciani, Jean-Dominique, 28

Maghrib, Arab conquest of, 6, 11, 60-61
Mahdī, Ibn Tūmart named as, 25-26
Mahdism, concept of, 26, 28-29
Mahdiya, Ifriqiya, 3, 82; siege of, 56-57
Mahyū, chief of Banū Marin tribe, 91
Maisara, revolt of, 112
Mālik ibn Anas, 62n
Mālikī school of law, 14, 53
al-Ma'mūn, Abū al-'Alā Idrīs, 94, 97
Manṣūr, al-, 71, 77, 79. *See also* Abū Yūsuf Ya 'qūb al-Manṣūr
Marinides tribe, 35
Marçais, G., 74n
Marrakesh, Morocco, capital of Almohad empire, 70, 89, 92; Almohad court in, 75-76; battle of, 39, 52, 93, 100; Ibn Tūmart's arrival in, 22-23; palace of, 63
Marrākushī, Al-, 6, 31, 65n, 80

Index

Maṣmūḍa, Berber group, 3-5, 13, 24, 26, 29-30, 32, 43, 48, 85, 87
Merad, Ali, 60n, 65n
Meunié, Jacques, 40n
Miranda, Ambrosio Huici, 3n, 5, 8n, 31, 34n, 61n, 70, 73n, 75n, 80n, 82n, 83n, 84, 92, 93n, 95, 97n, 100n
Mohammed, the Prophet, 45
Montagne, Robert, 4n, 33
Morocco, sultanate of, 3, 14, 20, 68; Arabs of, 79, 104
Muḥammad, son of 'Abd al-Mū'min, 67-68
Muḥammad ibn 'Abd Allah Ibn Tūmart, *see* Ibn Tūmart
Mulīn, Muḥammad Rashīd, 71
Mū'minid family, 68
Muslim civilization, new form of, 88
Mustanṣir, Yūsuf al-, 89-90
Muwaṭṭa', book of, 62

Nāṣir, Muhammad al-, 67, 80, 83, 86-87, 100
Navas de Tolosa, Las, *see* Las Navas de Tolosa, battle of
North Africa: Berber kingdom in, 57, 90; climate of, 111; political unity of, 57, 110-113. *See also* Berber tribes
Nfīs Valley, 27

Paul, St., 9

Qal'a, al-, city of, 11

Ragrāgī, Muhammad b. 'Abd al-Karīm al-, 81
Rashīd, al- (son of al-Ma'mūn), 97-99
Rawḍ al-Qirṭās (Ibn Abī Zar' al-Fāsī), 4n, 35, 61n, 65
religious reform, Ibn Tūmart's mission of, 6, 26-27
Revival of Religious Sciences (al-Ghazzālī), 14
Ribāt al-Fatḥ, Rabat, 76, 83, 108
"right path," 10

Sa'īd, al-, 99
Salvatierra fortress, seizure of, 84
Ṣanhāja, Berber tribe, 13-14, 30
Santarem, Spain, 70, 74
"Seven years' campaign," 52
Sevilla, Spain, 69, 70, 71, 76, 100, 107
Shleuh group, 3
Sijilmāsa, conquest of, 98
Spain: holy war against, 58-59; 'Abd al-Mū'min's occupation of, 55
Spanish civilization, in Almoravid empire, 12
Spanish kings, attacks by, 83, 98, 100, 102, 104, 109
Spanish Moslems, as conquered people, 13
Summān River, 16

Tasghimūt, fortress of, 39
Taza, mosques at, 63
Terrasse, Henri, 12n, 28n, 63n, 103
Théry, G., 70n
Tijānī, Al-, 82n
Tinmel (Tinmallal), community and fortress at, 27, 47, 50-51, 92, 102; military conquest in, 37; mosque of, 64
"Tinmel people," 32
Tlemcen, province of, 17, 19, 48, 51-52
Tornberg, C. J., 5n
Trara Mountains, 48
Tūmart, Ibn, *see* Ibn Tūmart
Tūmart, Isā (brother), 36
Tunis, 56

Umaiyad caliphate, 12
Umm al-Rabi' River, 100

Index

'Uqba ibn Nafi', 4

Valencia, Spain, 98

wird (spiritual exercise), 18

Yaḥyā ibn Ghāniya, Abū, 81, 99
Yaghmorāsan ibn Ziyyān, 99
Yūsuf ibn Tashfīn, 12-14, 75

Zainab (sister of Ibn Tūmart), 36
Zanāta group, 13
Zīrids, ruling family in Ifrīqiya, 87

GPSR Authorized Representative: Easy Access System Europe - Mustamäe tee 50, 10621 Tallinn, Estonia, gpsr.requests@easproject.com

www.ingramcontent.com/pod-product-compliance
Lightning Source LLC
Chambersburg PA
CBHW051528230426
43668CB00012B/1777
* 9 7 8 0 6 9 1 6 2 1 8 1 4 *